Also by Aleksandr Solzhenitsyn

August 1914 [The Red Wheel/Knot I]
Cancer Ward
A Candle in the Wind
Détente: Prospects for Democracy and Dictatorship
East and West
The First Circle
The GULag Archipelago
Lenin in Zurich
Letter to the Soviet Leaders
The Mortal Danger
Nobel Lecture
The Oak and the Calf
One Day in the Life of Ivan Denisovich
Prussian Nights
Rebuilding Russia: Reflections and Tentative Proposals
Stories and Prose Poems
Victory Celebrations, Prisoners,
and *The Love-Girl and the Innocent*
Warning to the West
A World Split Apart

"THE RUSSIAN QUESTION"

AT THE END OF THE

TWENTIETH CENTURY

Translated and annotated by

YERMOLAI SOLZHENITSYN

Including

ADDRESS TO THE

INTERNATIONAL ACADEMY

OF PHILOSOPHY

❧

FARRAR, STRAUS AND GIROUX

NEW YORK

"THE RUSSIAN QUESTION" AT THE END OF THE TWENTIETH CENTURY

ALEKSANDR SOLZHENITSYN

Library of Congress Cataloging-in-Publication Data
Solzhenitsyn, Aleksandr Isaevich.
[Russkiĭ vopros. English]
"The Russian question" at the end of the twentieth century
Aleksandr Solzhenitsyn ; translated and annotated by
Yermolai Solzhenitsyn. — 1st ed.
p.   cm.
Including "Address to the International Academy of Philosophy."
1. Russia (Federation)—History—1991–   2. Russia (Federation)—
Forecasting. 3. Russia—History—Philosophy. I. Solzhenitsyn, Yermolai.
II. Title.
DK510.76.S6513   1995   947.086—dc20   94-49411   CIP

"The Russian Question" was written in March 1994
and was first published in Russia in Novy Mir,
an important literary journal.
A portion of the "Address to
the International Academy of Philosophy"
first appeared in The New York Times.

Contents

"THE RUSSIAN QUESTION"

AT THE END OF THE

TWENTIETH CENTURY

T o d a y, if one desires to read anything at all, one wants it to be brief, as brief as possible, and only *o n   t h e   s u b j e c t s   o f   t h e   d a y*. But every moment of our history, including today's, is but a point on its axis. And if we wish to identify feasible and sure ways out of our menacing misfortunes, we must not lose sight of the numerous blunders in our past. Our plight today in many ways stems from these mistakes.

I realize that this essay does not propose specific practical measures for our immediate future, but I do not believe I have the right to offer such suggestions in advance of my impending return to Russia.

March 1994
Cavendish, Vermont

We cannot avoid a historical glance far back into our past, but will trace here only the correlation between our country's internal condition and her external efforts.

The existing myth of a flourishing **Novgorod democracy** in the fifteenth and sixteenth centuries is refuted by Sergei F. Platonov*. He portrays an oligarchy comprised of a small circle of the richest families, and argues that the predominance of the Novgorod elite had reached a level of political dictatorship. Mechanisms of compromise had not been honed and quarrels between feuding factions were played out, often bordering on anarchy, by throngs on the street. Platonov maintains that, in its rapid development, the social and political order in Novgorod had decayed significantly in its own right, even before it was broken by Moscow.

A democratic society did develop in the midst of the

---

* Sergei F. Platonov, *Smutnoye Vremya (Time of Troubles)*. Prague, 1924.

thriving and free peasantry of **Pomorye***, precisely *after* its liberation from Novgorod. (Moscow did not plant its landowners here, as it did not perceive any foreign threat from the north.) The Russian character developed naturally in Pomorye, uninhibited by Moscow's rule and without the inclination to maraud, a tendency notably adopted by the Cossacks of the southern rivers. (That the light of Lomonosov came to us precisely from Pomorye was no accident.)

In the **seventeenth-century Time of Troubles**[†], after all the ravages and depravations visited upon Russia and its people, it was none other than the Russian North, with the strong support of Pomorye, that served as the trusty rear first for Skopin-Shuisky's troops, and then for Pozharsky's volunteers, who brought lasting liberation and peace to Russia.

Platonov remarks that the torturous and enervative Time of Troubles brought also a beneficent change to the political outlook of the Russian people: even with no Tsar, with Russia no longer his "estate" and its people no longer his "servants" and "serfs", the State must not collapse, but must be salvaged and shaped by the people themselves. Local authorities grew stronger everywhere; local *mirs*[‡] passed resolutions;

---

* Area that straddles the southern and southeastern coast of the White Sea. Arkhangelsk is the chief city in the region. [Translator's note]

[†] An anarchic and lawless interregnum which lasted from 1605 to 1613. Drastically weakened, Russia became a battleground for Polish, Swedish and other interests. To fight against Polish-backed puppet governments, Russian militias were organised under Mikhail Skopin-Shuisky in 1606 and Prince Dmitri Pozharsky in 1611. The latter campaign ousted the Poles and culminated in the election of Mikhail Romanov as Tsar. [Translator's note]

[‡] The basic self-governing organisational unit of communal agriculture found in the Russian countryside from mediæval times until the twentieth century. Also known as *obshchina*. [Translator's note]

messages and emissaries flowed between cities; and socially representative councils sprang up in urban centres, uniting in turn to form a "council of all the land". (The sixteen-months-long stand of Troitskaya Lavra and the twenty-months-long resistance of Smolensk* are two examples of such independent action.) This testimony to the Russian people's organisational abilities provides instructive examples for us, the descendants.

Thus arose the *zemstvo*†, taking its place beside the Tsar; and **Mikhail** from the outset sought assistance from the *Zemsky Sobor*‡, which the latter readily provided. The Tsar's power was not formally limited in any way, but close ties linked him and "all the land". For the first decade of Tsar Mikhail's rule, the *Sobor* sat in continuous session; later it would convene periodically. (This entire system of State was not created under any Western influence, and by no means amounted to an imitative structure.)

Without delving into the latter reigns of the Rurik dynasty, let us recall that then also, side by side with the all-powerful Tsar, viable administrative institutions existed at the local level (even under conditions of extreme ignorance as to the concept of civil right), along with the elected posts of *starosta*§ in charge of criminal affairs, the head *zemsky starosta*‖, and the

* The Troitskaya Lavra is the famed Monastery of the Holy Trinity in Sergiev Posad, near Moscow. During the Time of Troubles it withstood a Polish–Lithuanian siege, 1608–10. The city of Smolensk, in western Russia, fell to the Poles in 1611. [Translator's note]

† A representative assembly of a given locality's entire population; a permanent institution from 1864 until the Revolution. [Translator's note]

‡ "Assembly of the Land", a national representative body convened in 1613. [Translator's note]

§ Generic term for a local elected official. [Translator's note]

‖ *Starosta* of a *zemstvo*. [Translator's note]

*zemskaya izba** (in charge of taxation, land allot-
ment, needs of settlers). One must note, however, that
landlord-owned serfs had minimal influence in these
institutions (although they were represented by the
sotskie†and *communal starostas*‡).§ The local structures
which played such a salutary role in the Time of Troubles did not, therefore, appear out of thin air. But the
military needs of the government tied the serfs ever
more securely to the lands of those gentry serving in
the army; and the peasants, seeking freedom, fled to
the sparsely populated periphery. The centre thus lost
people and labour, while the outlying regions wit-
nessed the rise of mutinous freemen. Both these trends
had disastrous effects during the Time of Troubles and
long thereafter: the three-to-four-century-long development of serfdom runs as a ruinous thread through
Russian history.

This *Sobor* period, however, was ending rapidly under **Alexis**, who through a bizarre historical quirk was
immortalised as "the Quietest". In his reign, the administrative approach to governing gradually gained
precedence over the *zemstvo* principle, and the healthy
resources of the latter were pushed aside by a poorly
organised bureaucracy for three hundred years to
come. His rule was replete with rebellions—the people's resistance to the rule of governors and administrators—and the Code of 1649 only deepened the
enslavement of the peasantry‖ (thus precipitating a se-

---

* Local government office, akin to a town hall. [Translator's note]

† Low-level law-enforcement officers. [Translator's note]

‡ *Starostas* of the *obshchinas*. [Translator's note]

§ Lev A. Tikhomirov, *Monarkhicheskaya gosudarstvennost'* (*Monarchical Statehood*). Buenos Aires: Russkoye Slovo, 1968.

‖ Sergei F. Platonov, *Moskva i Zapad* (*Moscow and the West*). Berlin:
Obelisk, 1926. Pp. 111–14.

ries of insurrections which culminated in the Razin
uprising*). The Polish war conducted by Alexis was
both necessary and just, for he was recapturing historically Russian lands usurped by the Poles. This military encounter revealed to him both our backwardness
vis-à-vis the West and the acute need to acquire Western knowledge and technology. Not to lag behind in
anything Western thus became a sort of "fashion",
even to the extent of introducing servile corrections
into canonical texts. This vogue led Alexis brutally
and criminally to subject his own people to anathema
and to wage war on them in the name of "Nikon's
reforms"† (even when Patriarch Nikon himself had
abandoned the "Greek project")‡. Forty years after the
people had barely survived the Time of Troubles, the
entire country, frail as it still was, was shaken to its
spiritual and vital foundations by the Church Schism.
And never again, during those same three hundred
years to come, did Orthodoxy in Russia regain its vig-
ourous dynamism, which had upheld the spirit of the
people for more than half a millennium. The Schism
would echo also in our weakness of the twentieth
century.

Then, upon this shaken people, upon this country
not yet healed, descended the wild whirlwind of Peter.

As a "servant of Progress", **Peter I** was a man of

---

* Cossack and peasant revolt (1670–71) led by Stepan (Stenka) Razin.
Razin was captured and executed in 1671. [Translator's note]

† In the 1650s, Patriarch Nikon undertook a series of ecclesiastical
changes to bring Russian religious practice and texts in line with those of
the Greek Church. The changes, widely viewed as needless foreign innovations, were met with fierce opposition and resulted in the bloody
Church Schism of 1666–67. The dissenters eventually came to be known
as Old Believers. [Translator's note]

‡ Sergei A. Zenkovsky, *Russkoye staroobr'adchestvo* (*The Old Believers
of Russia*). Munich: Wilhelm Fink Verlag, 1970. Pp. 290–339.

mediocre, if not savage, mind. He could not grasp that one cannot transfer specific results of Western culture and civilisation without the psychological atmosphere in which these results had ripened. Yes, Russia needed both to catch up to the West technologically and to gain access to the seas, especially the Black Sea (where Peter acted with a particular lack of talent, as when, to rescue his encircled army on the Prut River, he ordered Shafirov to relinquish Pskov to the Swedes via the Turks; Ivan L. Solonevich proffers some critically astute comments regarding Peter's military record*). Russia needed this, but not at the cost of stamping out (in quite a Bolshevik fashion and with many excesses) her sense of history, her people's beliefs, soul, and customs, for the sake of accelerated industrial development and military might. (We can see from mankind's recent experience that no material and economic "leaps" compensate for the spiritual losses borne in the process.)

Peter destroyed the *Zemsky Sobor* as well, "beating out all memory of it" (Vasily O. Klyuchevsky). He bridled the Orthodox Church, broke its spine. Taxes and duties rose out of proportion to the population's resources. Mobilisations stripped entire regions of the best craftsmen and land-tillers; fields became overgrown with forests; road construction stalled; smaller cities fell still; the lands of the North lay empty; and the development of our agriculture came to a halt for much time to come. As for the needs of the peasantry—this ruler did not feel them at all. If by the Code of 1649 the peasant was tied to the land, he

---

* Ivan L. Solonevich, *Narodnaya monarkhiya* (*Popular Monarchy*). Buenos Aires: Nasha Strana, 1973.

nonetheless had the rights of ownership, inheritance, many personal freedoms, and property contracts. But the decree of 1714 on gentry primogeniture turned peasants into the direct property of landowners.

Peter also created, for the next two hundred years, a ruling class if not always alien to the people ethnically, then always alien to them in world view. And then that demented idea of splitting the capital—to transfer it (what *cannot* be torn out and transferred) onto phantasmal swamps, and raise there to the wonder of all Europe a "paradise", to oversee the fantastical construction of palaces, canals and piers, but to do so with clubs, driving to death the masses already in such want of a respite. Between 1719 and 1727 alone, Russia lost, through death and flight, nearly one million people*—almost one in ten! (One can see why the belief that Peter was an impostor and the Antichrist firmly took root among the people. His reign rocked with rebellions.) All the great and not-so-great undertakings of this Tsar were carried out with no concern whatsoever for the waste of national energy and flesh.

One would be hard pressed to justify the view of Peter as a *reformer*; a reformer is one who takes the past into account and smoothes the passage into the future. In reforming government, writes Klyuchevsky, "Peter suffered the most setbacks". The failures and mistakes which he left behind would nonetheless "later be acknowledged as the sacred legacy of the great reformer", even though the decrees of his final years read as "vague verbose sermons".† Klyuchevsky passes

---

* Sergei M. Solovyov, *Istoriya Rossii s drevneyshikh vremyon* (*History of Russia from Ancient Times*), vol. XI. Moscow, 1963. P. 153.

† Vasily O. Klyuchevsky, *Kurs russkoi istorii* (*A History of Russia*), lectures, vol. 4. Pp. 190, 198.

a scathing sentence on the civic policies of this Tsar. Peter was not a reformer but rather a *revolutionary* (and, for the most part, without warrant for such an approach).

The eighteenth century rolled on after Peter, wasteful of national energy to no less a degree (and marked by the fretful twitches of the broken line of succession, with Peter once again to blame). After his feverish rule, writes Klyuchevsky, an "abyss" opened up, "a severe exhaustion of the nation's strength, with the people labouring under insupportable burdens". * One cannot agree with the widespread notion that the conditions presented by the aristocrats of the Supreme Privy Council to Anna would have been a step toward the liberalisation of Russia: too shallow ran this princely plough and never would it have tilled the nation's depths. German influence and even predominance increased sharply under Anna, while the Russian national spirit was trod upon in every sphere, land ownership rights of the gentry were solidified, serfdom further entrenched (now newly-established factories could buy peasants without land), the people subjected to heavy requisitions and to the squander of living strength in clumsily waged wars.

Anna's reign was distinguished by foolish, unsuccessful wars and a foreign policy to match. Peter, in his rash sweep, could concern himself with helping Prussia obtain Pomerania and Stettin; now his heirs bustled about for Denmark to annex Schleswig; and simply to obtain subsidies, Münnich volunteered to maintain a fifty-thousand-strong Russian force to put in the service of France, at her beck and call. Although manifesting no concern for the sizeable Russian, Be-

* Ibid., p. 304.

lorussian, and Malorossian* population lost to Poland,
Anna's government was nevertheless preoccupied with
the task of placing the Saxon elector on the Polish
throne. At a time (1731) when the Crimean Khan[†]
boasted that he "could cover Russia with a rain of
lashes"[‡] (while Tatar raids from the south had already
left a bitter taste in Russia and Malorossia, and could
always recur); at a time (1732) when Russia was hastily
retreating from the distant Persian conflict, abandon-
ing not only Baku, Derbent and the entire surrounding
regions (where Peter in his time had thrust out without
thought for a foothold or a calculation of strength),
but even Svyatoy Krest; at a time (1733–34) when
famine struck at home and the Bashkirs rose up in
rebellion (1735)—at that very same time (1733–34)
Anna began a war against Poland with the aim of
placing the Saxon elector on the Polish throne. (How
is this better than the Polish invasion of Russia during
the Time of Troubles and Sigismund III's plans to
seize the Moscow throne?) "Russians could not at all
understand the sense of the Polish war" (Sergei M.
Solovyov). Through this intervention, Russia managed
to erect against herself a front of France, Sweden,
Turkey and the Tatars, with only the faithless Austria
for an ally. Immediately (1734), the Tatars began to
attack Russian borders, while Russia (in fulfillment of
a treaty signed by Catherine I) was forced to dispatch
twenty thousand troops to aid Austria in Silesia. Inev-

---

* *Malorossia*, meaning Russia proper, comprises what is today central
and western Ukraine. [Translator's note]

[†] Ruler of the Crimean Khanate, the last vestige of the Golden Horde
(a mediæval Tatar empire). The Crimean Tatars continued to launch raids
into Russia during the eighteenth century. Russia absorbed the khanate
in 1783. [Translator's note]

[‡] Solovyov, vol. X, p. 282.

itably, in 1735, a draining war broke out with Turkey. Strategically, it was the only conflict in line with Russian interests, as we were suffocating without access to the Black and Azov Seas. But oh, how it was waged! Münnich's leadership was pitiable, exhausting for the troops and tactically feeble. Before even encountering the Turks, he lost half of his original force to the Tatars. With an infamous lack of skill, he stormed Ochakov (1737) from the least advantageous direction, neglecting an easy approach; captured it with enormous losses; and then proceeded to abandon it, changing his course to the southwest to aid the Austrians. Here, finally, he fought a successful campaign; but Austria betrayed him by abruptly concluding a separate peace with the Turks, forcing Russia to end the war by razing all the fortresses she had sacked: Ochakov, Perekop, Taganrog and Azov. But our heaviest loss was in men: 100,000 dead. Russia's population at the time was 11 million (smaller than a century before, under Alexis; thus had Peter thinned it out!). And let us picture the lives of those recruits: there was no set term of service; soldiers were enlisted, in effect, for life; the way out was death or desertion.

As for the spiritual condition of the Russian people by that time, we look to Solovyov's assessment: "The lower clergy, drowning in poverty and in hard agrarian toil, had no opportunity to stand out from their flock in any educating capacity", and this predicament of the clergy "brought terrible moral harm to the masses".*

He refers to Anna's reign as the darkest of all—for the complete dominion of foreigners over Russia had summarily suppressed the Russian national spirit; only

---

* Ibid., p. 547.

during **Elizabeth**'s rule did it begin to recover. (However, contempt for the Russian essence, for all things native, for the faith of their *muzhiks*, saturated the ruling class throughout the eighteenth century.) But here we shall focus on the other events and trends of Elizabeth's rule.

Before acceding to the throne, she played a very risky and morally dubious game with French and Swedish diplomats in St. Petersburg. France counted upon Elizabeth to establish a *Russian* reign, return the capital to Moscow, shift her attention away from naval concerns and Western affairs, and thus lead Russia off the European stage. Elizabeth carried on dangerous discussions with Sweden concerning a declaration of war on Russia (the former subsequently obliged in July 1741), and urged her to demand the restoration of Peter's dynastic lineage. (The Swedes, on the other hand, demanded the restitution of all the territories annexed by Peter, a concession Elizabeth refused to consider.) However, the Elizabethan coup in St. Petersburg was eventually executed without the assistance of either France or Sweden, and the new Empress ascended the throne with her hands untied.

True, in Elizabeth the Russian national feeling was alive, and her faith was by no means a pretence (as it would be with Catherine II). Before assuming the throne, Elizabeth made a vow, in prayer, never to resort to capital punishment; and, indeed, during her reign not a single death sentence was carried out—a highly unusual phenomenon for the Europe of that time. She softened punishments for numerous different crimes. She declared an amnesty (1752) for all arrears accumulated over the previous quarter-century—since the death of Peter. Elizabeth "soothed the wounded feelings of a people ruled by foreigners for many years", and "Russia returned to her senses". She strained several times (1744, 1749, 1753) to bring the capital back to Moscow; she transferred the entire court there for periods of as long as a year, and commenced renovation of the Kremlin. Her Russian feeling demanded thus, and yet her filial sense forbade Elizabeth to undermine the designs of her father. Nonetheless, she was not consistent and did not move far in alleviating the plight of the people. Senseless and cruel persecutions of Old Believers (they responded by setting themselves on fire) continued in her time—an extermination of the Russian root itself. Peasants languished under new taxes: from Vyatka they ran off to form secret settlements in the woods, from the central provinces they fled across the Polish border (though to a humiliating and wretched existence), while Old Believers sought to preserve their faith beyond the Dnestr. The total number of such fugitives approached *one million*! Labour became scarce everywhere and the authorities applied significant efforts to return the fugitives from beyond the Don. Peasant uprisings erupted in the Tambov, Kozlov and Shatsky districts, and entire villages fled to the lower Volga in search of freedom. Numerous insurrections flared up also among peasants tied to monastery lands. (How unseemly it was for the monasteries to exploit peasant labour.) It was no coincidence that in 1754 Pyotr I. Shuvalov proposed a plan for the "preservation of the people": to free from conscription those peasants paying a poll tax; to distribute stored bread to settlers in cases of poor yields, and conversely, to raise the price of bread in years of plentiful harvests so as to protect villagers from losses incurred through a decline in price; for designated adjudicators to mediate in disagreements between landowners and peasants; to curtail bribe-taking among officials, while raising their salaries; to protect settlers from plunder and oppression, sometimes at the hands of the army; to provide for and educate the soldiers' young; and even "for the benefit of the state" to conduct "a free study of society's opinion". Elizabeth, however, had gained the throne with the support of the gentry Guards and remained intangibly dependent on them, thereby strengthening, to use Klyuchevsky's phrase, "the rule of gentry". (Thus, in 1758 the landowner gained the right to monitor the behaviour of his serfs; in 1760—to deport his serfs to Siberia. At the same time, the requirements of military service for the gentry, as in Anna's reign, were further mollified.)

And yet, despite the grave condition of the state and the century-long exhaustion of the people, the wavering Elizabeth, instead of "preserving the people", concerned herself with "threats to the European balance", and unforgivably threw Russia into European quarrels and dubious ventures, so alien to us. Having swiftly and resoundingly defeated the Swedes, Elizabeth keenly pursued the preposterous idea of placing one of the Holstein princes in line for succession to the Swedish throne (but what monarchs of the age did not weave grand politics around dynastic marriages and calculations?), and with that in mind in 1743 she ceded Finland, which had been freed from the Swedes, back to Sweden (thus letting slip the possibility, beneficial to Russia, of Finland's free development; independent *diets* had already existed there in the seventeenth century). She was then further drawn in: to protect Sweden from Denmark, the Russian navy was dispatched and infantry was sent to Stockholm— why spare them? . . . (And for two decades to come, the Russian government was intensely occupied with

Sweden's internal affairs, provided funds for the security of our empty "alliance", bribed deputies in the
Swedish Diet, and Russian diplomats in that country
passionately strove "to ensure that autocracy is not
restored" in Sweden, so that she might remain weaker.)
Some also yearned for a close alliance with Denmark,
but were blocked by the Holstein pride of the heir to
the throne, Peter. In similarly reckless fashion, Elizabeth took on burdensome and entirely disadvantageous obligations to England (1741), from whom
Russia had never seen any goodwill or assistance, and
entered into a direct alliance with her (1743), thereby
committing Russia to act in England's interests on the
European continent (based on that deepest of calculations: the Swedo-Holstein prince *would* after all wed
the English queen, and what a coalition we would
forge then! The perceptive Austrian chancellor von
Kaunitz reported to Maria Theresa in 1745: "The politics of Russia flow not from her true interests, but
from the individual inclinations of specific persons").
And then in 1751 Russia made a secret promise to
defend the private territories of the English king in the
Principality of Hanover—in the west of Germany, just
around the corner! Monstrous!

Next to us, growing ever more impotent from gentry
discord, lay Poland. In the preceding centuries she had
annexed and oppressed a large Orthodox population,
but it was not the latter's welfare that troubled Elizabeth; rather: how to maintain the integrity of the weakened Poland (after all, our beloved Saxon elector was
on the Polish throne), and at the same time continuously to defend Saxony. (Why should any of this have
concerned us in the least?) In the early years of her
reign, Elizabeth understood that an alliance with Austria could bring us no benefit whatsoever. But suddenly

Prussia, the martial and enterprising Frederick II, took Silesia away from Austria; Elizabeth then forgave Austria (for plotting against her), renewed (1746)—for another twenty-five years!—the outdated treaty with her, and sent Russian troops through independent Poland to protect Austria and Saxony from Frederick! Yes, Frederick acted with naked aggression, but Russia still lay very far removed from any threat or danger. Even had he taken Poland, would Frederick ever have dared to invade the enormous expanses of Russia?

At this stage our finances are in ruins, there is a shortage of recruits, and yet we send troops to counter Frederick (while our own roads and rivers, for lack of garrisons, are ridden with thievery); but he, having obtained what he desired from Austria, makes peace. Is our campaign then for naught? No! we still manage in 1747 to send a thirty-thousand-strong army beyond the Rhine, to the Netherlands, helping Austria and gratuitously antagonising France. (Who can fathom such an expedition? . . . Yet we do not hear the grumble of the soldiers and the people.)

At least peace descends upon all of Europe (but Russia is not invited to the congress at Aachen, and receives nothing at all). To recompense us, history records that Russia's intervention brings the War of the Polish Succession to a halt, ends the War of the Austrian Succession, and stops the impudent Frederick in his tracks.

But he is not stopped for long: keeps poking about Europe, conquering. And in 1756 Russia insistently attempts to convince Austria together to strike at Prussia as soon as possible (while England clashes with France in America). In the meantime, we "do not possess one decent general" (Solovyov), because, under Anna, Russian generals were not reared, the mil-

itary being in the hands of German mercenaries.
Austria stalls, Frederick takes Saxony with lightning
speed, and the Russian army trudges abroad for the
Seven Years' War (with promises: exactly what to restore to Austria, what to Poland; but to Russia—nothing). Elizabeth pined for the "gratitude of the Allies
and of all Europe for the security provided them"
and urged on her four talentless oft-replaced field-
marshals. (It must be admitted that from St. Petersburg
she assessed her positions more clearly than her marshals did, even taking into account the time delay of
messenger travel.) War was waged as follows: summers
(not all) were spent in combat, and early autumn saw
a timely retreat far back from enemy lines to peaceful
winter quarters. (In Prussia our troops compensated
the population for all material losses.) The war revealed many shortcomings in the training and condition of the Russian armies. Our generals knew how
to place their troops in battle facing the sun and a
sand-filled wind (battle at Zorndorf). In all the major
engagements Frederick attacked first, but the Russians
either stood firm or attained victory, and by 1757 were
already on Prussian soil. Frederick took flight after the
battle of Kunersdorf (August 1759)[*], deeming not only
his campaign, but his very life, lost for good. The
Russians entered Berlin in 1760, but left in two days
without securing the city. This time Elizabeth wanted
a piece of Prussia, not for its own sake, but rather to
trade it to Poland for Courland; Austria and France
strongly resisted, however, and the venture was
blocked. Meanwhile, the Crimean Khan persistently

---

[*] Kunersdorf, a town on the right bank of the river Oder, is now Ku-
nowice, Poland. The Seven Years' War battle here (also called the Battle
of Frankfurt-an-der-Oder) set the stage for the Russian occupation of Berlin. [Translator's note]

incited Turkey (England was nudging her as well) to start a war with Russia (and how would Russia have held out?); Turkey wavered, but after the battle at Kunersdorf refused. The Seven Years' War lulled in 1761 (especially on the Austrian side). Strength and resources required to maintain the Russian army in its distant campaign continued to dwindle; we now asked England to mediate for peace with Frederick, while the latter, exhausted but fully aware of the circumstances, would not budge. And then—Elizabeth died.

Her nephew ascended the Russian throne. He was a nonentity, a man of meagre and shallow mind, whose development stalled at a childlike level, a soul of Holstein mettle—the madcap **Peter III**. "Gentry rule" was further entrenched by his 1762 decree "on gentry freedoms", dooming Russia for the next hundred years to be weighed down by the governmentally nonsensical burden of serfdom. (As one result of this decree, the army lost many officers and was forced once more to fill its vacancies with foreigners.) "He resolved to change our religion, which he regarded with particular disdain", ordered icons to be removed from churches, and priests to shave their beards and wear clothes akin to those of foreign pastors. (Conversely, a positive edict was issued to cease persecution of Old Believers, Muslims and idolaters.) The most important turnabout effected by Peter III in his half-year reign, however, was in foreign policy: he suggested that Frederick II, who had lost the war and was ready to cede Eastern Prussia, *himself* draft a treaty to benefit Prussia. Peter offered to return all territories occupied by Russia, and even to enter into an immediate Prusso–Russian alliance. He further agreed to help Prussia against Austria (transferring General Chernyshov's sixteen-thousand-strong corps to Frederick for this purpose) and dispatched Russian forces in Pomerania against Denmark to recapture Schleswig for his native Holstein. (The Guards' unwillingness to campaign once more, this time against the Danes, was instrumental in bringing closer the hour of Catherine's coup.) "The deeds of Peter III deeply offended the Russian people . . . they smacked of mockery at the blood spilled in the struggle", [*] and not only did Peter surround himself with men of Holstein and Prussia, but all of Russia's foreign policy was directed by the Prussian Ambassador Goltz. The Russian people "looked with despair to the future of the motherland, now in the hands of talentless foreigners and ministers of a foreign sovereign". [†]

Catherine's coup, unlike Elizabeth's, was by no means a splash of Russian national feeling. Judging by Catherine's initial impulsive efforts, though never realized, to lay down a Code (her *Ukaz* of 1767 spoke of *rights* so expansively and with such audacity, so daringly did she "sow the European seeds" of her time, that it was *banned* in pre-revolutionary France), one could have expected that she would do much to raise the people's condition, and protect, to some degree, the rights of the oppressed millions. But only minor steps were taken: a slackening of the pressure on Old Believers, the issue of instructions not to use excessive force in quelling peasant uprisings. (Catherine proved more generous to the German colonists invited by her: distribution of extensive tracts of land, construction of houses for their use, liberation from taxes and all service for thirty years, and interest-free credits.) "To help poorer landowners make ends meet", she continued

[*] Solovyov, vol. XIII, p. 58.
[†] Ibid., p. 66.

to expand ever more the rights of the gentry, who were not satisfied even with the decree "on gentry free-doms". The right of each landlord to deport his serfs to Siberia (later, even to hard labour) without providing any reason to the judge was confirmed. (The land-owner could deduct such a serf from his recruit quota as well.) "The landowner traded him [the serf] as a live commodity, not only selling him without the land . . . but tearing him away from his family".* Perhaps worse yet was the plight of peasants sent to work in factories (quite often far away from their homes and with few days in the year set aside for them to work for themselves). In addition, Catherine "granted" to her favourites, or those she was rewarding, up to one million souls of hitherto free peasants, and laid down stricter regulations of serfdom in Malorossia, where the peasants previously had the right to move between landowners. The commission working on the Code had planned to grant the gentry boundless power over the peasants (in effect this was already the case, even in the administrative sense), and not to accept from serfs any complaints about their masters. During her trip to the Volga in 1767, several peasant complaints did find their way to the Empress, causing her to issue an order "henceforth not to file any such like", and per her instructions the Senate ruled "that peasants and other servants shall by no means lodge complaints against their landowners", with violators to be whipped. Peasants working in factories were to "enter into silent obedience under threat of severe punish-ment".† Catherine even sent armed detachments across the Polish border to retrieve forcibly the peasants

---

* Klyuchevsky, vol. 4, p. 319.
† Solovyov, vol. XIV, pp. 54–56.

who had fled. The pages of Solovyov's detailed *History* provide us with numerous depictions of extortion at the local level. The deputies assembled by Catherine declared: "He who can—plunders". Did Catherine grasp all this? She was surrounded by boundless flattery and falsehood, which pleasantly screened her from the grim life of her people. Our renowned poet Derzhavin, who held major posts under three Emperors and was a close observer of life at the court, wrote: "Catherine's soul was occupied more with political glory and political designs . . . She ruled the state and administered justice more by political and personal convictions than by the holy truth . . . She ruled politically, keeping an eye on her interests, or indulging her nobles."*

She was particularly embittered by Pugachov's uprising (1773–74).† In response to Pushkin's phrase (uttered in passing, but since then repeated and carelessly thrown about, especially by the *obrazovanshchina*‡ of our time), "the Russian riot, senseless, with no mercy", Solonevich fairly counters: why all that "senseless"? Eleven years after the decree on gentry freedoms (indeed a senseless one from the state's perspective), and with Catherine's rule waxing oppressive, was there truly no reason to rise up? In Pugachov's manifesto we read: "catch [the gentry], execute and hang them, and do unto them in like manner as they,

---

* Gavriil R. Derzhavin, *Sobranie sochineniy* (*Collected Works*). Annotated by Ya. Grot, 2nd academic edition, vol. VII. St. Petersburg, 1878. Pp. 627–32.

† Peasant and Cossack rebellion led by Yemelian Pugachov. Pugachov's armies were defeated, and Pugachov himself executed in 1775. [Translator's note]

‡ Coined by Solzhenitsyn in the 1960s, *obrazovanshchina* refers to the lower strata of Soviet intelligentsia, who, though possessing a formal education, lack spiritual and intellectual depth. [Translator's note]

having nothing Christian in them, have done unto their peasants . . . and when these gentry adversaries and villains are rooted out, all will feel a peaceful and calm life, which will last for all time". Did Pugachov himself believe this? "Freedom" he imagined to be a collective arbitrariness of the majority, and he possessed no concept of an organised and structured freedom (S. Levitsky). But "having nothing Christian in them"—it's true! It is characteristic that in Pugachov's uprising, as in the insurrections of the Time of Troubles, the masses never yearned for anarchy, but were taken in by the lie (as later with the Decembrists) that they were acting for the good of the true Tsar. Is that not why Pugachov easily captured cities, even Saratov, Samara (which greeted him with bells ringing), and was joined by Old Believers in Irgiz? (Incidentally, Derzhavin, who served in the areas of the uprising, notes the arrogance, stupidity, and perfidy of the nobles charged with putting down Pugachov's rebellion.)

On the other hand, believing herself to be a progressive European, Catherine was all the more acutely interested in the problems of Europe. Not yet secure on the throne, she was forced to swallow Peter III's shameful peace with Prussia, but then (1764) entered immediately into an entirely disadvantageous alliance with her, and subordinated herself to Frederick's agenda. Jointly they schemed to place Poniatowski on the Polish throne (aimless efforts: Klyuchevsky believes that, due to the peculiarities of the Polish constitution, a friendly Polish king was as useless to us as a hostile one was harmless; and once elected, Poniatowski began to betray his patrons and grew friendly with the French king). For many years Nikita Panin wooed

Catherine with the fruitless project of a *système du Nord**, one that could only benefit England (it never formed; for that matter, no assistance could ever have come to us from England, Sweden or Denmark. England, in turn, was brazen enough to demand, in 1775, that Russia send twenty thousand men to Canada; the Empress, however, sanely refused.)

Catherine was prudently concerned that the Orthodox population in Poland "come into legal status in terms of rights and justice", of which it had none. Despite Russia's great influence in an eighteenth-century Poland weakened by internal strife, these Orthodox were being subjected to coercive Polonisation (a serious omission of Peter I, who did not address this problem at all; nor did Elizabeth). Catherine was able to secure some protection for them, although she feared that greater rights would tempt even more Russian serfs to flee west. (In reaction to concessions in Poland, Polish officials and the Uniate clergy began arbitrarily to persecute Orthodox peasants in the Ukraine, which led in 1768 to a terrible *haydamak* uprising, to much cruelty and death. Its cry was: "For the faith!", and it too was screened by the monarch's shadow through a forged Imperial decree†). The presence of Russian troops in Poland and scattered skirmishes with Confederate units‡ led to unease in

---

* The concept of a Northern Alliance—to include England, Denmark, Sweden, Prussia and Russia—serving as a counterweight to the Franco–Austrian alliance. It was espoused only briefly by Catherine II. [Translator's note]

† The 1768 rebellion of Orthodox *haydamaks* (Turkish for "marauders") against Polish rule was abetted by a forged "Golden Manifesto" sanctioning it. [Translator's note]

‡ Polish Catholic rebels who derived their name from the Confederation of the Bar, 1768. They fought against Catherine II's forces, but were defeated in 1772. [Translator's note]

Turkey, who at the time shared a border with Poland. The attack of one *haydamak* detachment on a Tatar settlement near Balta afforded a direct excuse: in September 1768, Turkey (egged on by England and France in every conceivable way) declared war on Russia (and caught her unprepared). Soon after, Khan Krym Girai with his seventy-thousand-strong force was pillaging and burning Elizavetgrad province (the last Tatar invasion in Russian history, 1769). Poland welcomed with great enthusiasm Turkey's attack on Russia; its consequence was the cession of Kiev province with its Orthodox peasants to the Ottoman Empire.

Here Catherine committed several serious diplomatic blunders. She counted Prussia for an ally; expected Austria, in the face of Muslim Turkey, to act favourably towards Christian Russia; and pursued the goal not only of gaining access to the Black Sea (the single objective of *vital* importance to Russia then) but of "setting fire to Turkey from four sides". She conjured up the unrealizable "Greek project": to restore the Byzantine Empire on the ruins of the Ottoman (Voltaire also suggested Catherine take up this plan; already she was marking her grandson, Constantine Pavlovich, for the new throne), dispatched fleets to Greece (rounding all Europe), and sent agents and instigators to the Balkan Christians. This chimerical plan could not have approached realization, it was even impossible to raise the Greeks to such a project —but, for the first time, the sinister spectre of Russian intervention in Balkan affairs flitted across Europe.

Alas, this false, hollow and accursed idea impelled both the Russian rulers and, later, Russian society for the duration of the nineteenth century—quite naturally setting all of Europe (and especially Balkan neigh-

bour Austria) against us for the century and a half until
the First World War.

The campaign unfolded quite auspiciously for Russia: Azov and Taganrog were taken; Bucharest fell by
the autumn of 1769, Izmail by 1770; major battles
were won near Fokshany, the Kagul River, near Ches-
men, and even Beirut was captured from the sea; in
summer 1771, Russian troops were in the Crimea;
Kerch was taken. But despite this string of successes,
concrete results remained elusive. Russian military
victories were undermined diplomatically: once again,
European diplomacy proved unpredictable and insol-
uble for Russia's diplomats. Russia's "ally" Frederick,
remembering well the harsh lessons of the Seven Years'
War, now strove through the final treaty to bring Russia's victories to naught. The Russo–Turkish war did
much to bring Prussia and Austria closer together. The
latter would not accept the independence of Moldavia
and Walachia (Russia had hoped this would weaken
Turkey by cutting off her land route to the Tatars),
but on the contrary was eagerly eyeing them for herself.
Had Russia successfully advanced towards Constantinople, Austria was prepared to strike at her back (a
scenario which would recur in the nineteenth century). Meanwhile, Russia's resources were sorely depleted. In addition, her troops in Turkish-controlled
regions were falling to the plague (which then spread
to Moscow and wrought great destruction because city
residents did not understand and disregarded the necessities of quarantine). Peace talks began with Turkey
in 1772, but were at first unsuccessful (Turkey was
wavering); peace was not concluded until 1774 (the
Treaty of Kuchuk-Kainarji), when a new Sultan came
to power and the rising Suvorov won several battles.
This treaty preserved the independence of the Crimean

Tatars, but acknowledged their religious subordination to Turkey. Russia advanced in the steppe (initially to the Dnestr River, later only as far as the Bug River), and acquired the shores of the Azov Sea, Taman and Kerch. Moldavia, Walachia and the Zabuzhye* remained under Turkey. Russia was also allowed to act as patron of the Orthodox faith throughout the Ottoman Empire. (At the time, this patronage was sincerely understood in a religious sense only—but a dark political shadow was cast onto the future, and the European Powers, from whence the Crusades were once launched to Asia Minor, henceforth took it upon themselves unanimously to protect Turkey from Christian Russia.) But in fact, the war was not yet over: sensing the support of Europe, Turkey vacillated in fulfilling the treaty, and by 1779 Russia made further concessions, withdrawing from Taman and the Crimea.

In the meantime, the keen-witted Frederick espied the convenience of splitting up Poland against the backdrop of the bloody Russo–Turkish war. (He had entertained this plan before. To give her credit, Maria Theresa deemed such designs to be un-Christian, and debated the matter at length with her son and heir, Joseph. Finally, "the Viennese court, in order to diminish the injustice of the partition, saw it as its duty to take part in it".) In fact Austria received the largest chunk of Poland, and took a portion of northern Bukovina from Turkey (the latter being more than willing also to take part in the partition). "Golden Russia" (Galicia and Transcarpathia), the heritage of Kievan Rus'†, was also handed over to Austria. By that first

---

* Area southwest of the Southern Bug River. [Translator's note]
† The East Slavic state of the ninth to twelfth centuries. Its capital was Kiev. [Translator's note]

partition Russia regained her long-lost Belorussia, while Frederick took lands of Poland proper. But the Polish state, reduced as it was, continued to exist.

The years 1787–90 saw yet another war with Turkey; Russia yet again had Austria for a faithless ally, and, unexpectedly for Russia, Austria yet again made separate peace. Russian forces, in the meantime, yet again achieved major victories: at Bendery, Akkerman, at that same elusive Ochakov; then the decisive sacking of Izmail by Suvorov. As her victories amassed, Russia sensed yet again that the European Powers would not let her reap the fruits of success. England declared that she would not abide any alteration of the Turkish borders (this at a time when Turkish territory extended as far as the Southern Bug and the lower Dnepr Rivers!). Prussia had entered into a secret alliance with the Sultan in preparation for war. The Powers met in congress (Reichenbach, 1790), which was to be the sole arbiter and maker of the Russo–Turkish peace. (Spain, the Netherlands and Sicily were eager to lend a helpful hand in the process.) But paradoxically, the French Revolution halted these plans: with Europe scared stiff, Russia seized the moment to conclude (1791) a victorious peace at Jassy. (Klyuchevsky writes that the previous war with Turkey would have ended on similar terms had Europe not intervened.)

Thus Russia reached a natural southern boundary: the Black Sea (including the Crimea) and the Dnestr River (in much the same way as she had already reached the Arctic and Pacific Oceans). We should have known to stop at that—after four eighteenth-century Russo–Turkish wars. Alas, in the next century Russia would fight four more wars with Turkey, no longer justified by national sense or state interests.

The enfeebled Poland was twice more partitioned

(1792 and 1795) behind the protuberances of the French Revolution. Russia took Volyn', Podolia, the western part of Belorussia (lacking only Galicia to complete the unification of the Eastern Slavs or, as they were referred to at the time, of the *Russian tribe*, the heritage of Kievan Rus'). "Russia took nothing of Poland proper, but rather recovered her ancient lands, plus a section of Lithuania".* Prussia, on the other hand, took indigenously Polish territory, including Warsaw.

Here again von Kaunitz noted that Catherine was obsessed with exerting influence in the West, and had a maniacal proclivity to interfere in the business of others. (One example was, to use Klyuchevsky's assessment, the "most absurd" treaty with Austria in 1782: to form a non-existent "Dacia" out of Moldavia, Walachia and Bessarabia, to place Serbia and Bosnia under Vienna, and to give Peloponnesus, Crete and Cyprus to Venice.) Derzhavin writes that "towards the end of her life [Catherine] thought of nothing but the conquest of new kingdoms". Her intervention in the Franco–Austrian conflict was not only fruitless but harmful. Catherine had conducted six wars (one of our bloodiest reigns), and was before her death preparing for a seventh—against revolutionary France.

Unfortunately, **Paul I** *did* wage this war. Suvorov's heroic expeditions in Italy and Switzerland, which so capture our imagination (and that of the Swiss, to this day), were in fact *absolutely unnecessary* for Russia, amounting only to the squander of Russian blood, strength and resources. Equally unnecessary was the opposite thrust: to join Napoleon in fighting England, with the insane plan of sending the Don Cossacks to

* Klyuchevsky, vol. 5, p. 60.

India (this undertaking cost six million rubles, according to Derzhavin*; and there is more than well-grounded suspicion that the plot to remove Paul was nurtured from England).

There are contradictory assessments of Paul's personality and brief reign. Klyuchevsky calls him an "anti-gentry Tsar", and Trefilov writes that Paul "took to heart the needs of the serfs". And true, one cannot but value that, on the day of his coronation (1797), he decreed that no serf must work directly for his landowner in excess of three days a week, and must "not be made to work on Sunday"; in 1798, Paul forbade the sale of serfs without the land to which they were tied: this edict was an important turning-point for serfdom, which slowly began to recede. He also revoked Catherine's law forbidding serfs to lodge complaints against their masters, and introduced complaint boxes. But, as an inside observer, Derzhavin writes (not without a personal grudge) of Paul's lack of balance, of his recurring failure thoroughly to grasp matters at hand (in meetings where contradictory plans were presented, he ruled: "it shall be thus"); also that during Paul's reign, structures established under Peter and Catherine were mangled without warrant, and many were even "put to grief on account of calumny"; that upon assuming the throne and at his coronation, Paul "quickly and with poor judgement" gave away "left and right . . . state serfs belonging to the court", at times taking from them the best state lands, "even those under cultivation". Of Paul's circle, Derzhavin writes, "none concerned themselves with anything touching the common good of the country, but rather pursued personal luxury and benefits". (This charge,

* Derzhavin, vol. VII, p. 718.

of course, can be leveled against the elites of different countries at various times—not only autocratic, but even the most democratic—to our very day.)

Pausing at the end of the eighteenth century, one cannot but marvel at the string of errors committed by our rulers, at their concentration on matters superfluous to the life of the people. In his day, Lomonosov had warned: "We can have only one war against Western Europe—a defensive one". Already by the end of the seventeenth century the people longed for a lengthy respite, yet for still another century they were not let alone. It would seem that now all the external tasks of national importance had been fulfilled; to pause now, then, and concentrate entirely on internal welfare? No! the external ambitions of Russia's rulers remained far from sated. It would seem, to use Solovyov's words, that because of the expanse of the Russian state, not only did "the desire to acquire foreign belongings not develop among the Russian people" (among the people, no, and yet among the rulers?), but "lack of desire for others' possessions could even turn into lack of attention towards one's own", and it did . . .* Daniil S. Pasmanik makes a related observation: because of Russia's expanse, the people easily developed in a horizontal direction, yet did not grow vertically for that very same reason. "Wild heads" and "critical personalities" went off to the freedoms of Cossack life (while Western Europe huddled in cities and built up culture); and Russia's rulers felt the itch of colonisation rather than the intensity of concentration.

Unfortunately for us, this mindset persisted long into the nineteenth century. And our eighteenth and

---

* Solovyov, vol. XIII, p. 438.

nineteenth centuries in essence fused together to form the *St. Petersburg period.*

Contemporaries and historians agree on the personality of **Alexander I**: a romantic dreamer who loved "beautiful ideas" and then grew weary of them, a "will fatigued before its time", an inconsistent, indecisive, unconfident and many-faced man. Influenced by his tutor La Harpe, a Swiss revolutionary, he lent "exaggerated importance to forms of governing" (Klyuchevsky), readily considered and participated in developing a liberal constitution for Russia (for a society half of which was enslaved), then granted a constitution to the Kingdom of Poland a century before Russia obtained its like. He freed priests from corporal punishment (monstrously still in use!), permitted serfs to wed without the landowner's consent, and halfheartedly leaned towards emancipation, albeit without any intention of providing peasants with land (like the Decembrists, incidentally). He changed nothing in this respect, however, with the exception of the 1803 "Law on Free Land-Tillers" (allowing for their liberation with the landowner's approval, and forbidding further distribution of state peasants to the latter). He showed leniency towards the activities of secret societies, himself at a young age privy to a fateful plot*. "Indiscriminately bad-mouthing the reign of Emperor Paul, they began indiscriminately to butcher all that he accomplished", writes Derzhavin concerning the Tsar's entourage, which "was full of French and Polish constitutional spirit," and while "the young gentry were allowed to indulge in idleness, comfort and willfulness, the enemies of the fatherland were under-

---

* Alexander I was at the very least apprised of the plot to remove his father, Paul I, in 1801. [Translator's note]

mining the strongest defences of the state". By 1812, he recounts, the highest dignitaries "had brought the state to a disastrous condition".* Bureaucracy contin-ued to burgeon under Alexander I.

True, Western Europe was reeling and breaking, Napoleon was crushing and creating states, but this should not have concerned Russia, with her peripheral location, her expanses (daunting to any conqueror), and her population in such dire want of rest and of a ra-tional and caring administration. W h y did we need to get involved in European affairs? Yet Alexander I did precisely that, neglecting internal Russian matters. (He strongly resembled Catherine in his preoccupation with Western ideas.) French historians see it as follows: Alexander I was surrounded by pro-English advisers and began a needless war foisted on him by England, forming a coalition with Austria (1805) and Prussia (1806) to fight Napoleon. We squandered so many lives in those unnecessary battles, squandered that "desperate courage of Russian soldiers, which the French could not even have imagined". Alexander I could not now forgive Napoleon for Austerlitz and gathered fresh forces against France. War loomed with Turkey and Persia—but no, Alexander was preparing for a lengthy campaign: to throw Napoleon back be-hind the Rhine. At this stage, an agent of Napoleon convinced the Sultan to declare war on the Tsar.†

Taking umbrage at Britain's indifference, Alexander then flung himself into friendship with Napoleon: the peace of Tilsit (1807). One cannot but acknowledge the exceptional wisdom of that move for Russia at the

---

* Derzhavin, vol. VII, pp. 723–53.

† Ernest Lavisse, Alfred Rambaud, ed., *Istoriya devyatnadtsatogo veka* (*The History of the Nineteenth Century*), vol. 1. Moscow: OGIZ, 1938. Pp. 125–40.

time. She should have held to this line of friendly and neutral relations, disdaining the grumblings of St. Petersburg's high-society salons (which, incidentally, were capable of a new pro-English plot) and of land-owners, who could not export grain due to the Continental Blockade (more would have been left for Russia). Yet here again Alexander was wary of inaction. No, the Tilsit peace and the brewing conflict with Turkey were insufficient: in that same year (1807) he declared war on England. Napoleon "offered Finland", and Alexander promptly moved in (1808), taking her from Sweden—w h y ?—yet another unbearable weight placed upon Russia's shoulders. He did not want peace with Turkey if it meant withdrawing troops from Moldavia and Walachia; again we find Russian troops in Bucharest (Napoleon "offered" Moldavia and Walachia to Russia, and even suggested that she split Turkey with France, thus opening for himself a route to India); and after a coup d'état in Constantinople, Alexander craved more ardently than ever to advance on Turkey. But instead of all these fevered conquests, why not keep to the Tilsit peace (so advantageous for Russia), avoid entanglement in the European melee, and grow stronger and healthier within? However wide Napoleon's expansion in Europe (although bogged down in Spain), he had not yet raised up his sword against Russia (only persisted in drawing her into vexatiously sprightly alliances), and as late as 1811 sought to avoid confrontation with the Tsar. *The Patriotic War could have been avoided!*— all its glory, but all its losses, too—if not for the missteps of Alexander. (While the Persian conflict stagnated for another year, we, almost miraculously, dragged ourselves out of the war with Turkey through the efforts of Kutuzov, one month before Napoleon's invasion. The Turkish conflict was not extinguished in 1809 because Alexander demanded Serbia's independence—the kindling of the pan-Slavic idea! . . .)

With utmost exertion and with Moscow in ashes (it is a little known fact that fifteen thousand Russians wounded at Borodino* burned to death in Moscow hospitals[†]), we won the war. So now, then, to stay inside our borders? (Such voices *were* heard among the generals.) No, Russia must help to bring the European house to order (and thus create two future enemies—the mighty empires of Austria and Germany). After the battle of Lützen[‡], "Alexander could have obtained anything he wished through a separate peace with Napoleon", but the "thought of Russian interests drowned in this self-styled mission to bring about world peace", while "we lost an entire army on the fields of Lützen, Bautzen, Dresden, Leipzig and others, fell hundreds of millions into debt, devalued the ruble . . . even to the rate of twenty-five kopecks in silver, and complicated our development for decades to come".[§] (And during "The Hundred Days" we magnanimously dispatched 225,000 men; enraged, Alexander now resolved to wage war "to the last man and ruble".) Did Alexander drive the Russian troops on to Paris guided by monarchical considerations—to restore the Bourbon throne? No, he wavered on this issue to the last (Talleyrand convinced him), then

---

* The 1812 Battle of Borodino (near Moscow) was hailed by Russians as a great moral victory. [Translator's note]

† Lavisse, Rambaud, vol. 2, p. 269.

‡ A pyrrhic victory for Napoleon, in 1813. His army was decimated after this battle. [Translator's note]

§ Klyuchevsky, vol. 5, pp. 454–55.

demanded that the Bourbons swear to uphold the constitution*, and conveyed his liberal outlook to Louis
XVIII. Was he seeking territorial rewards for Russia
after such a bloody and victorious war? No, he did
not put forward any preconditions whatsoever for aid-
ing Austria and Prussia in 1813. The single wise move
he could have made was to return Galicia to Russia,
thus uniting the Eastern Slavs (and from what disastrous problems would he have rid our future history!).
Austria was not particularly bent on retaining Galicia
at the time, seeking rather to regain Silesia, annex
Belgrade and Moldo-Walachia—thus stretching herself between the Black and Adriatic Seas. But Alexander did not make use of this opportunity, although
it was then easily within his grasp. No, hopelessly
infected with "beautiful ideas", and not seeing, if only
through Austria's example, how harmful it is for the
dominant nation in a state to create a multiethnic
empire, he demanded that Russia receive the central
region of a further repartitioned Poland. Having annexed this Grand Duchy of Warsaw, he could now
pour down his personal grace and care onto the "Kingdom of Poland", add to it several Russian provinces,
bestow upon it a progressive constitution—and in return, for a century to come, obtain for Russia yet
another poisoned gift, another rebellious nest, another
burden on her shoulders, and yet another reason for
Polish antipathy towards Russia.

Our wars with Persia, meanwhile, already had a
lengthy history, their main purpose being the defence
of Georgia. As far back as the reign of Boris Godunov,
the Georgian Tsar (Alexander) had sought Russian
patronage, and in 1783 Tsar Erekle II made a similar

---

* Lavisse, Rambaud, vol. 2, pp. 351–52.

plea. (Due to religious notions, it was considered natural and essential to help a Christian people pinned against the far side of the Caucasus Range; here, too, the interests of the Russian state and people were relegated to the background.) During her last year on the throne, Catherine ordered a forty-three-thousand-strong force to Azerbaijan (Paul recalled it). Alexander renewed this undertaking, and occupied Dagestan—*for what benefit to Russia?* to navigate the landlocked Caspian Sea? Before Tilsit, Napoleon also prodded the Persian Shah to invade Georgia; after Tilsit, it was England who did the prodding. The peace of 1813 ceded Georgia and Dagestan to Russia—a dangerous entanglement in ever new and unnecessary traps.

During the second half of his reign, Alexander I lapsed into conservatism. The soul of the Holy Alliance, he went as far (1817) as to demand that the request of the Spanish king be satisfied by sending troops to put down the rebelling South American colonies—one place the Russian troops had not yet managed to reach! (Metternich talked him out of it.) In 1822 Alexander heatedly proposed to quell revolution in Spain itself. On the other hand, he was prepared to support with Russian troops a Christian (Greek) revolt against the Turks and held negotiations with England regarding joint action. Then came that which is called his decease*.

Nicholas I believed that he was first and foremost a *Russian* sovereign, placed Russian interests above the common interests of the European monarchs, and therefore distanced himself from the Holy Alliance. But this unbending enemy of revolutions could not

---

* Alexander I's death is shrouded in mystery. Legend has it that he departed to a life of seclusion and prayer. [Translator's note]

hold back: in 1830 he was ready, and began convincing the German monarchs, collectively to crush the July revolution in France and then in Belgium (the Polish uprising threw this plan askew); likewise in 1848 he offered the Prussian king the use of Russian troops to suppress the Berlin revolution; in 1848–49 he actually did send sizeable detachments on a mission both harmful and alien to us: rescuing the Habsburgs from the Hungarian revolution. Nicholas then again supported the Habsburgs against Prussia (1850)—with what benefit to Russia? incomprehensible! if one delves into numerous other details, our constant bailing out of Austria looks even more absurd. (In gratitude, Nicholas was stabbed in the back by her in the Crimean War.) In 1848, he sent troops to put down disturbances in Moldo-Walachia, acting in concert with Turkey against a Christian populace . . . We had to mind everyone else's business. And during the long era of Nesselrode, Russian diplomacy remained just as giftless and improvident, failing to act strictly in Russian interests.

The persistent malevolence with which the entire Russian liberal society (alas, including Tolstoy) regarded Nicholas I throughout the nineteenth century (a spitefulness repeatedly played up by the Bolsheviks) flows mostly from his suppression of the Decembrist uprising*. (Pushkin's death was also pinned on Nicholas with little hesitation.†) Today one all too easily

---

* A coup staged soon after the death of Alexander I in December 1825 by a group of disgruntled officers. The officers demanded political liberalisation and insisted that Alexander's brother Constantine be made Tsar. Constantine, however, had already refused the throne. [Translator's note]

† Pushkin died in a duel with Baron Georges Hecheren d'Anthès in 1837. There have been speculations that d'Anthès acted in concert with court interests hostile to Pushkin. [Translator's note]

dismisses that certain aspects of the Decembrists' programme promised Russia a revolutionary tyranny, and
that some Decembrists insisted during their inquests
that freedom could only be built upon corpses.
(Equally, let us not gloss over the following details.
Nicholas came out of the Winter Palace to face an
agitated crowd; was shot at together with his brother
Mikhail; General Miloradovich was killed . . . and
still Nicholas refrained from ordering warning shots to
be fired. It would seem that, with our Soviet experience, we ought to appreciate: a l l the lower-ranking
officers were pardoned within four days; there was no
distortion, nor was pressure brought to bear during the
interrogation of the 121 officers arrested; of the thirty-
six sentenced to death by the court, Nicholas pardoned
thirty-one. And on the day the five were executed, a
manifesto concerning the kin of the condemned was
made public: "The tie of kinship passes down to descendants the glory of deeds wrought by ancestors, but
stains them not with dishonour for personal flaws or
crimes. Let no one dare reproach them for their kinship". [If only this were so in our Soviet age . . .] And
when the Polish Sejm pardoned the local Decembrists
on the basis of its *own* law, a livid Nicholas, respecting
the *law*, assented.)

We find an external assessment of Nicholas in the
writings of nineteenth-century French historians: "Dil-
igent, precise, hard-working . . . thrifty"* (this last
quality was sorely lacking in our Emperors after Peter,
including Catherine). He stood apart from many of his
predecessors precisely in his persistent search for State
wisdom and in his understanding of Russian interests.
But the totality of power he held over a vast empire fos-

---

* Lavisse, Rambaud, vol. 3, p. 163.

tered in him, as the years passed, an exaggerated belief in what he could achieve through his *will* alone—a misjudgement further coarsened by his inflexibility, leading to the misfortunes at the end of his reign.

In the meantime, serfdom, which, since Peter III, had already for seven decades made little sense as far as the State was concerned, continued to expand, notes Klyuchevsky, to cruel and unwise lengths, impeding the development of agriculture as such, harming the country's productivity, and retarding societal and intellectual development. "The new Emperor possessed the courage to tackle the peasant question upon ascending the throne", "the thought of liberating the serfs occupied the Emperor in the first years of his reign", but "changes were considered carefully and in silence", "secretly from society" (in apprehension, as it were, of strong gentry resistance). "Difficult enough when approached one at a time, these reforms taken together made for a turnabout, the full brunt of which could hardly be borne by any single generation". The Emperor faltered in the face of warnings from his circle. But a "reform which slackens excessively loses many of the conditions for its success". Nicholas "meticulously searched out men who could complete this important task", and his choice fell on Count Pavel D. Kiselyov, "the best administrator of the age".* Kiselyov, having gathered an exceptionally enlightened team, was put in charge of the 17–18 million state-owned peasants (there were also 25 million privately-owned serfs in a country of 52 million), was given the right to buy out peasants from the landowners and to take them away in cases of cruel treatment. Energetically he set to work. There followed the pro-

* Klyuchevsky, vol. 5, pp. 272, 275, 460–61.

hibition on splitting peasant families through sale (1841), the ban on the acquisition of peasants by landless gentry (1843), and other laws (concerning buyouts and the acquisition of real estate, 1842 and 1847) easing the peasant lot. "Taken together, these laws were designed fundamentally to alter how [serfs] were viewed": "that a serf is not simply the property of a private individual, but is first and foremost a subject of the State", and that "personal freedom ought naturally be obtained by a peasant, and need not be purchased". *

But our accursed serfdom, with which the gentry so cozily cohabited in their poetic estates, and which permeated the souls of millions of peasants, would weigh on Russia for yet another decade and a half.

Continuing the efforts of Alexander I to support the Greek uprising against the Turks, Nicholas I, soon after assuming the throne, issued an ultimatum to Turkey (1826), and maintained this tone despite the start (also 1826) of war with Persia, securing (through the Akkerman Treaty of 1826) a further consolidation of Russian rights and trade in Turkish ports, as well as promises for Serbia (our "Balkan idea" was growing stronger . . . His tendency to spring headlong into action led Nicholas I into many blunders). Having assisted Russia in 1827 (the battle in Navarin Bay), England and France joined the rest of Europe in cocking an attentive ear to the Sultan's cry that "Russia is the eternal and indomitable enemy of Islam, plotting to destroy the Ottoman Empire" (itself significantly weakened by the elimination of the Janissary corps in 1826). It would have been prudent for the Russian Emperor to desist. But under insignificant pretences,

* Ibid., pp. 273, 278–79.

and increasingly setting Europe against himself with declarations of "Russian interests" in Moldavia, Walachia, and Serbia, Nicholas launched another war with Turkey in 1828. The campaign unfolded propitiously along the Caucasian coast (from Anapa to Poti), in Transcaucasia (Akhaltsikhe, Kars, Erzurum, and as far as Trabzon, in Turkey proper), but ran into setbacks in the Balkan theatre. (Our troops were better in drill than in combat, could not afford rifled arms, and had inferior reconnaissance, though in his analysis of the war the elder Moltke praises the great endurance of the Russian soldier.) True, in 1829 we passed through Bulgaria (where, to our Slavic surprise, the Bulgarians were not friendly at all in their reception), and took Adrianople (Turkey was shaken), but then our momentum petered out. We secured independence for the Greeks, the vassalage (to Turkey) of Serbia—again, the interests of others—and free passage for Russian ships through the Bosphorus. In this Turkish war (our sixth!), Russia attained her greatest military successes and yet there was now n o t h i n g e l s e left for her to gain.

And what is more, four years later Nicholas undertook to s a v e Turkey from the successfully rebelling Pasha of Egypt: a Russian fleet rushed to Constantinople to aid the Sultan. Russian interests again . . .

Meanwhile, we freed Armenia through our war with Persia.

The responsibility for Georgia and Armenia taken on by Russia compelled her to lead a new, protracted (sixty years!) and bloody war: the conquest of the Caucasus. Had Russia not become involved in the alien lands of Transcaucasia, she would have had no need to assert control over the range itself. Keeping a strong line of Cossack defences along the northern foothills

would have been sufficient to repel the constant
thieving forays of the mountain peoples; the Caucasus
was not a single state but rather a multilingual assem-
blage of various tribes and did not in itself pose any
threat to Russian security, especially after the enfee-
blement of Turkey. (There was even a moment when
Nicholas was prepared to recognise Shamyl's kingdom;
yet the latter, a Caucasian temperament, declared that
he would reach Moscow and St. Petersburg.) But
throughout the nineteenth century we continued and
continued to pay and to pay the bills of others . . .
The expenses of maintaining the Caucasus and Transcaucasia, up until the Revolution, were greater than
the profits derived therefrom: the Russian Empire *paid*
for the joy of possessing these territories (while nowhere, notes Klyuchevsky, "breaking local customs").

A similar problem arose with Khiva and Bukhara,
which regularly attacked Russia's southern borders as
late as the 1830s and 1840s: two strong states lodged
deep in the desert, holding numerous prisoners in
slavery, including Russians delivered through Turk-
men and "Kirghiz" (Kazakh) raids as far as the lower
Volga. Those abducted were sold at the slave markets
of Khiva and Bukhara.* We had either to establish a
strong line of defences against these raids—or to
launch a conquest. (There loomed, then, a path to
India? . . . yet would that not imply confrontation
with England?) Pursuing the latter option in 1839–
40, Perovsky led a thousand-kilometre trek through
the desert; he did not succeed.

In 1831, and then again in 1863, Russia paid for
Alexander I's dreamily absurd venture to keep Poland
under his "guardianship". How little feel for the time,

* Lavisse, Rambaud, vol. 4, pp. 373–76.

the age, one had to have, to hold subordinate within the Empire a people as cultured, developed and intense as the Poles! (Both Polish uprisings aroused much sympathy in Western Europe and brought new enmity and isolation upon Russia.)

Nicholas' diplomacy under Nesselrode dashed about incoherently for decades: an agreement (1833) with Austria and Prussia to fight the revolutionary movement; later that year, a defensive alliance with Turkey promising to protect her from any internal or external danger (irritating the Western Powers—the first seed of the future Crimean War); a secret agreement (1840) with England: in matters relating to Turkey, Russia will only act when and if empowered by Europe (why tether ourselves with these commitments?); then (1841) Russia refuses to guarantee before the Western Powers the territorial integrity and independence of the Ottoman Empire; from 1851 Russia heatedly intervenes in a superficial row (exacerbated also by a personal quarrel between Nicholas I and Napoleon III) between Catholics and Orthodox as to who holds primacy over the holy places of Palestine, a disagreement rapidly turning into an all-European political confrontation. —Nicholas confided to the English ambassador: "Turkey is a sick man", and may die at any moment; in the eventuality of Turkey's partition, let England take Egypt and Crete, while Moldavia, Walachia, Serbia and Bulgaria will find their independence under the patronage of Russia, rather than within her borders—for it would have been dangerous further to enlarge the already expansive Russian Empire. (This he understood, but the pan-Orthodox and pan-Slavic ideas were disastrously propelling him towards expansion in a different form.) The Russian ambassador in Constantinople, meanwhile, was demanding that the issue of the holy places be solved and that Russia become the official protector of the entire Orthodox population in the Ottoman Empire. But when the English ambassador to Constantinople began skillfully to settle the dispute over the holy places to the satisfaction of all parties, the Russian ambassador demanded "within a five-day period inviolable guarantees" of protection for the Orthodox, and then left the city with threats.

Clearly, the Russian government did not understand that because of Russia's rise over Europe after the victory of 1814, England had become her enemy for a century to come. Now Russia was setting *all* of Europe against herself. Let us not forget that our free passage through the Straits had been guaranteed by Turkey since 1829; what more did we require? (Besides, in case of a European war, anyone could plug up the Dardanelles from the outside.) But half a century after gaining access to the Black Sea, Russia had still not managed to build a strong, modern (at least partially steam-driven) navy there, having only sailers in those waters (not to mention that we were unable, for lack of skill and infrastructure, to bring the Black Sea coast under the plough. All across the expanses of Russia, unsolved, bungled and neglected affairs cried out and groaned for remedy.) Nor did Nicholas I fathom the degree of the technological and tactical backwardness of our army: loose order was not used; trenches were not employed; the cavalry was more accustomed to riding school than to battle. He also ignored the mounting animosity of Russian society towards his administration (thus surfaced, for the first time, the phenomenon of *wishing defeat* upon one's own government), but was convinced he could rely on Austria and Prussia . . . (Meanwhile, Austria was threatened by Russian envelopment from a third flank; England was growing increasingly uneasy over Russian consolidation on the Syr Darya; as a newly crowned Emperor, Napoleon III sought an opportunity to prove himself; Victor Emmanuel II hoped to raise Sardinia's status among the European states; Turkey was experiencing a rise in patriotism supported by Egypt and Tunisia; and Prussia effectively joined the coalition in its demands.) And yet with astoundingly arrogant self-confidence Nicholas rushed to place his head in the noose! He declined several offers to negotiate. (He should have learned the lesson of 1790 and recognised this most dangerous configuration of all the European Powers against Russia.)

The course of the war is well known. After Russia's major naval victory over the Turks at Sinope, the Anglo–French fleet entered the Black Sea. We did not even try to hinder the Allied landing at Eupatoria (although it was widely predicted in the British press) nor did we, before the siege of Sevastopol (unfortified from land), make use of our enormous superiority in cavalry and our sizeable advantage in the number of bayonets—but rather marched about in formation under strong French fire. (The French, incidentally, saw a Russian "enemy possessed of the rarest military qualities, fearless, persistent, not one to lose heart, but on the contrary, after every defeat rushing into battle with renewed vigour".*) The Austrian threat forced the Russian command to abandon the Balkans and Moldo-Walachia. Sevastopol dug in, under Todleben, and withstood an eleven-month siege, until August 1855.

But half a year earlier, in February 1855, Nicholas I died (not without an element of mystery). The ascent

* Lavisse, Rambaud, vol. 5, p. 212.

of a new ruler always brings a shift in policy, a dramatic turnover of advisers, and after the pointless battle at the Chyornaya River (where our casualties ran at four to one), **Alexander II** began to succumb to the enfeebling advice to capitulate.

With historical hindsight, it is clear that starting the Crimean War was an act of self-assured madness. But after two years of hostilities, after the staunchness of Sevastopol's defence, and after so many were lost—should we have slackened so? The garrison of Sevastopol withdrew in full order to the well-fortified north side; though at a numerical disadvantage, it was forbiddingly steeled by the lengthy siege. Our Crimean army was well stocked both with ammunition and with provisions (every soldier received one pound of meat per day), was not severed from the Russian heartland, and thus could endure a second winter campaign. There was a dearth of good roads leading down to the Crimea, but this would only have complicated the Allied task of advancing further (especially as their naval line of communications had already extended to the length of four thousand kilometres). Besides, "due to considerations of national pride, the Allies were not united under one command, but the three armies had three separate general headquarters throughout the war", coordinating every operation with each other as if engaging in diplomacy. "The English, accustomed to conditions of great comfort, found themselves entirely unprepared for the severe climate; their enterprise and spirit faltered . . . mortality was horrifying: of the 53,000 troops arrived from England, only 12,000 remained battle-ready"* by spring 1855. After Russia's withdrawal from the Bal-

* Ibid., pp. 212, 220.

kans, Austria no longer threatened hostilities, and large Russian reserves were in any case positioned on the Austrian border, as well as in Poland, in the Caucasus, and by the Gulf of Finland (while the Baltic fleet successfully repelled Allied attacks at sea). By spring 1856, Russian armed forces were up to 1.9 million more numerous than at the start of the war. Solovyov (who in 1851, incidentally, was forbidden to give public lectures on Russian history) spoke of a "dreadful peace, the likes of which had not been concluded by Russian rulers since Prut" (the demeaning peace signed by Peter). He believed that "in order to make the Allies themselves end the war, we should have announced precisely at *this* stage that the war is not over but is in fact only beginning".* A struggle for Russian territory (assuming the Allies were still capable of moving further inland) could have rekindled in Russians the spirit of 1812, while Allied morale would inevitably have faltered.

This hasty peace of 1856 (by which Russia lost the Danube delta and the right to maintain her navy in the Black Sea) marked both an ill beginning for Alexander II's reign and the first victory of public opinion. (Russian liberals feared any successes of Russian arms, which could only bolster the government's strength and self-confidence, and were relieved at the fall of Sevastopol.) Taken together—all this was a precise and ominous glance into the future of 1904. (Alexander would later remark: "I committed a base act by making peace then".†)

But Alexander carried through the peasant reform with an atypical energy (given his usual "cautious

* *Russkiy Vestnik*, May 1896.
† Lavisse, Rambaud, vol. 5, p. 227. Annotation by E. Tarle.

anxiety"), relying on the power of his limitless autocracy in the face of gentry resistance. A secret committee on peasant affairs began its work in 1857, at first neither informed about conditions in the countryside nor possessed of a plan—to liberate the peasants together with the land or without it? Peasants belonging to the state and to the Imperial House were absolved from quitrent in summer 1858, thus obtaining economic freedom (they already had personal independence). Vagueness and uncertainty plagued the work of the reform commissions, characterised by protracted arguments as to who should receive the land, and whether the peasant *obshchinas* ought to be preserved; finally, Alexander demanded that the Emancipation Act be drafted by the sixth anniversary of his accession. The decisive step finally was taken (1861), but with glaring mistakes. Thirty years later Klyuchevsky wrote that "new beginnings of life emerged. We know these beginnings, but we do not yet know the consequences wrought by them".* Indeed, a l l the consequences made themselves felt only in the twentieth century.

Land was partially left in the possession of landowners (in deference to their stiff resistance), partially given to the *obshchinas* (with a Slavophile faith in them . . .), and only homesteads remained the private property of peasants (a foreshadowing of Stalin's collectivisation? . . .) The allocation (varied in different regions) of land to the peasants was both insufficient and costly for them: they were required to buy out "gentry" land (a concept they could in no wise grasp), and had nowhere to turn to for this money, as they had always paid for everything with either their labour

---

* Klyuchevsky, vol. 5, pp. 283–90, 390.

or its product. Moreover, in some cases the price fixed for the land significantly exceeded the profit that could be reaped from it, and was beyond peasant means. To finance the buyouts, the government now provided *loans* at six percent annual interest (with deferred payment over forty-nine years), covering four-fifths of the required amount; interest on these loans accumulated over the years, adding to the tax burden. (It was only the events at the beginning of the twentieth century that cut short the accretion of these debts and the succession of these forty-nine years.) In some places, peasants were still compelled to fulfill temporary obligations to the landowner. In many cases, *liberation* took away a peasant's right to the use of forests and common pasture. The Emancipation Act of 19 February granted personal freedom, but the possession of land and its fruits was more important to the Russian peasant than personal freedom. Many peasants were puzzled and bewildered by the Act (disturbances flared up occasionally), and waited for *another*, more generous measure. (Western historians, however, offer this assessment: "Despite all its limitations, the Russian reform turned out to be infinitely more generous than similar reforms implemented in the neighbouring countries, Prussia and Austria, where the serfs were offered an 'entirely barren' freedom, without the smallest strip of land".*)

The communal structure of the reform left the peasantry, in effect, without *full* personal freedom and disjoined from other social strata (e.g., a separate system of jurisprudence). To facilitate the realization of reform, the institution of *arbiter* (drawn from the local gentry) of peasant disagreements was temporarily in-

---

* Lavisse, Rambaud, vol. 6, p. 73.

troduced. The reform, however, failed to create an important nexus of administrative guardianship, which might have helped the peasants over the course of many years to complete the difficult psychological transition to an entirely novel way of life. With his hands still tied by the *obshchina*, the stunned peasant was thrown into the *market*. The brunt of taxation still weighed down on him, and without financial resources, he fell into the hands of shameless usurers and speculators. With reason Dostoyevsky anxiously wrote of the post-reform period: "We live now in perhaps the most transitive and fateful time in the history of the Russian people". (With even greater justification, this assessment can be applied to our day.) He saw that "the reform of 1861 demanded utmost care, but the people encountered only the estrangement of the higher social classes, and—the barkeeper." Furthermore, the "morally dark sides of the old order—slavery, alienation, cynicism, venality—grew stronger, while nothing remained of that order's positive sides".

The highly underrated and deeply sincere Gleb Uspensky, an astute observer of peasant life in the post-reform period, paints us a similar picture (*The Rule of the Land, The Peasant and His Labour,* 1880s). He believes that after 1861 there was "no heed paid to the masses", "no organisation of peasant life", while the predatory instinct had become firmly, and perhaps irreparably, ensconced in the village. Administrative and bureaucratic injustice continued to weigh heavily upon the peasant (the cry of the "Bonds of Injustice" chapter). Uspensky cites Herzen's lengthy quotation about a mysterious power preserved by the Russian people, a power which Herzen nevertheless does not attempt to define. Uspensky does: it is the *rule of the land*, and it is this rule which gave our people patience,

humility, strength, and youth; take it away and there
is no people, no national world view, only a spiritual
void. The people survived two hundred years under
the Tatars and three hundred years of serfdom because
it maintained its agricultural way of life. This rule of
the land held the peasant in obedience, developed in
him a strong family and social discipline, kept him
from pernicious heresies; the despotic rule of the earth-
mother went together with her "love" for the peasant,
thus easing his labour and making it the prevalent task
of life. "But this mysterious and wonderful rule did
not save the people from the blow of the ruble." (Due
to the integrity of his vision, and contrary to his revolutionary democratic consciousness and even party
membership, Uspensky could not refrain: under serfdom, the peasant was better placed in relation to the
land than he is today. Landowners' serfs had twice the
land they have now, and the landowner had to support
his peasants in all that made them tillers of the land.
In the days of serfdom, even army recruitment was
more just: the drunkards and good-for-nothings were
drafted first, then children from large families, leaving
no lumpen in the village to hamper the agricultural
labour of the peasant. Under the old economic system,
taxation also was fair: the rich always paid more than
the poor. "Our forefathers knew their people, wished
it well, and gave it the best that mankind has achieved
through centuries of suffering—Christianity. But today, we are rummaging through some kind of stale
national and European trash, through heaps of gar-
bage." Likewise, "church schools in the village were
charged with the task of turning an egoistic heart into
an all-grieving one. The education of the heart was
insistent, even tyrannical, but sought to instill severity

towards oneself and towards others, rather than emphasise benefits and unnecessary knowledge.")

But now a new epoch thundered the *blow of the ruble!*—considerations of *profit* and only profit! Our patriarchal peasantry, already buckling under the many injustices of the reform, could not withstand this abrupt change. Many writers of the post-reform period have left us descriptions of this constraint on the spirit, confusion, drunkenness, unbridled mischief and disrespect towards elders. (On 16 March 1908 fifty peasant deputies declared unanimously in the State Duma: "Let them take the vodka back to the cities if they want it, but in the villages it is summarily destroying our youth".) To all this was added the lowly position of the Orthodox clergy and the decline of the Orthodox faith. (Old Believers, meanwhile, preserved it, showing what we might have been if not for Nikon's reforms; in Leskov's *Cathedral Folk* we read of savage methods used in combating Old Believers even into the nineteenth century.) By 1905 and 1917 all this flowed organically into a revolutionary mindset and rebellion.

The quality of peasant labour declined towards the end of the nineteenth century. Available woodlands grew thinner and, in detriment to agriculture, dung mixed with straw was used as fuel. (Historians note that, at the time, fewer resources were invested in agricultural training in our country than in the study of Ancient Greek and Latin.) The poll tax was abolished in 1883, but *zemstvo* collections increased. By the beginning of the twentieth century the decline of agriculture in central Russia was becoming evident: the plough and harrow often made of wood, winnowing with shovels, bad seeds, the three-field system forcibly constrained by the *obshchina* in allocating to a peasant several nonadjacent strips of land, middle-men buying up produce practically for nothing, horses growing scarce, arrears continuing to accrue. In those years was coined the troubling expression—"the impoverishment of the Centre". (Platonov very aptly employs this same phrase, albeit in a different context, to describe the period leading up to the Time of Troubles in the seventeenth century . . .) Alexander's unfinished land reform had to be continued by Stolypin, but was met by a wall of opposition from the Right, from the Constitutional Democrats, Socialists and inefficient peasants; the entire process was then smothered by the Revolution . . .

Social stratification dangerously persisted in Russia after the reforms, as we can glean from the incomplete nature of judicial reform. When both parties in a dispute were peasants, small rural courts based on village traditions continued to function; above them were the arbiter judges who presided over civil cases and minor criminal offences; the next famed rung introduced by the reforms was entirely borrowed from the West, with prosecutor and defending attorney, permanently appointed judges, independent lawyer organisations, and the jury system. The latter is in general rather a dubious acquisition, for it diminishes the professionalism of the court (in contrast to the value modernity places on professionalism), at times leading to paradoxical incompetence (one can find examples of this in today's sufficiently decrepit court system in Britain). Post-reform Russian society imbibed with delight the discourses of attorneys (printed without censorship), which, along with the verdicts, bordered at times on tragicomedy. (Dostoyevsky vividly remarks: "the Bar is a brilliant institution, but somehow a sad one as well";

we might also recall the ominous acquittal of the terrorist Vera Zasulich, a promising glimpse of early dawn for the avidly desired revolution.) From these attorneys' speeches arose the convenient tradition of transferring the blame from the individual criminal onto the "accursed Russian reality".

The most fruitful of Alexander II's reforms was the introduction of the *zemstvo*—a permanent self-government organ with a wide range of executive functions and possibilities, surpassing even French local rule in scope.* This structure did not extend, however, to the lowest level of government, the *volost'* (a failure painfully felt in the twentieth century, in World War I). And in district *zemstvos*, elections of peasant deputies passed under the influence of local officials. (Dostoyevsky observes: "No one supports the people, and they have been left to fend for themselves. There is the *zemstvo*, but it is more like 'the authorities'. The people elect their representatives in the presence of some 'member', himself an official, and the elections turn into a farce".) Futhermore, the *zemstvos* lacked sufficient government subsidies, and to raise funds they would often impose higher taxes, thus becoming yet another parasite in the peasants' eyes.

Alexander III, seeking to pinpoint the administrative link neglected in his father's reforms, introduced the position of *zemstvo* official (1889), "a strong power close to the people", to act as the (extremely belated) guardian of peasant life who could smooth this laborious transition from the old traditions to the new, and help to put peasant activities and undertakings in good order. This post was filled from the reserve of idle gentry (from whom else to select?), often not at all

* Ibid., vol. 6, p. 81.

committed to the task; and thirty years after an incompleted reform these officials frequently constituted yet another burdensome layer of authority over the peasant (as when elected peasant courts were disbanded and the *zemstvo* official became the sole arbiter of disputes). Alexander III committed a serious mistake with the abrogation (1883) of the clause in the 1861 Emancipation Act allowing those peasants who bought out their land in full to opt out of the *obshchina*. For the sake of the *obshchina* idol, which fettered the Russian consciousness from the Emperor across to the *narodovoltsy** (the latter searching for ways to knock off the former), the path of free development for the most energetic, healthy, and industrious peasants was blocked.

Replacing Nesselrode, who had muddled our foreign policy for forty years, Gorchakov at first quite sensibly announced, in 1856, that Russia must concentrate on herself in order to "gather strength". We should long before have understood and abided by this precept. But these intentions did not last even a year: Russia once more immersed herself in the diplomatic games of Europe. With the blood not yet dry on the enmity with Napoleon III, **Alexander II** suddenly (1857) exchanged it for warm friendship. Through Gorchakov's demarche (1859) Russia prevented the German Confederation from taking Austria's side in the Italian war, while France helped Russia to oust Austria from its occupying positions in Moldo-Walachia (which soon united to form Romania) and to solidify Russian influence (just how vital for us?) in the Balkans. But because of the Polish uprising (1863), France turned against us, joining England and Austria

---

* Members of the terrorist group Narodnaya Volya (the People's Will). [Translator's note]

(a resurfacing of the Crimean War coalition?) in supporting the rebels, once again raising the spectre of war. Prussia, however, declared herself to be our friend, and obtaining our goodwill and neutrality in return, Bismarck proceeded to take Schleswig-Holstein from Denmark (1864), and stunningly smash Austria (1866); meanwhile, by remaining steadfast in our benevolent neutrality despite this increase in Prussia's strength, we ensured Bismarck's rout of France in 1870–71. (For this service, Russia was cunningly repaid by him at the 1878 Congress of Berlin: Bismarck joined the bloc of European states set on taking away from Russia the fruits of victory over the Turks.) Russian foreign policy under Alexander II remained myopic and unprosperous. In 1874 we find Dostoyevsky exclaiming: "For almost a century now, Russia has decidedly been living not for herself, but for Europe only" (*A Raw Youth*, Chapter 3). (By that time, "a century and a half" would have been more accurate.) For Europe only? in 1863, Russia did not miss the opportunity to use her fleet to aid the American North against the South—to what wise end? perhaps to take revenge on England?

Two wretched ideas relentlessly tormented and pulled all our rulers in succession: to help and to save the Transcaucasian Christians, and to help and to save the Orthodox in the Balkans. One can acknowledge the loftiness of these moral principles, but not to the extent of total disregard for the interests of the State, not to the extent of neglecting the needs of our own, also Christian, people. While we always sought to help the Bulgarians, the Serbs, the Montenegrins, we would have done better to think first of the Belorussians and Ukrainians: with the weighty hand of Empire we deprived them of cultural and spiritual development in their own traditions, and sought to "abolish" the hardly abolishable distinctions between us, which arose from the thirteenth to the seventeenth centuries. There is some truth in the reproaches leveled at Russian ruling and intellectual elites for their belief in Russian exclusiveness and messianism. Even Dostoyevsky, despite his incomparable acumen, failed to resist this subjugating influence: the dream of Constantinople, "the East will bring salvation to the West", and even disdain for Europe (an opinion which for a long time now has been impossible to read without shame). Need anything be said then of the woeful "all-Slavic" and "Constantinopolitan" conceptualisation of Nikolai Ya. Danilevsky in his book *Russia and Europe* (which is, incidentally, quite interesting in itself), a work almost unnoticed when it first appeared in 1869, but one that would strongly resonate in Russian society after 1888?

With the accumulation of national fatigue over three centuries, with our economic and social problems, with the "impoverishment of the Centre", with the menacing growth of bureaucratic willfulness incapable of high efficiency yet suppressing independent activity (we read: "the Russian character withered, daring and multi-talented personalities were harder and harder to find"; indeed, how many such characters are depicted in nineteenth-century Russian literature?), with all this—the endless wars for the Balkan Christians were a crime against the Russian people. Defending the Balkan Slavs from pan-Germanism ought not have been our task; while every forced incorporation of newer and newer Slavs into Austria only weakened this patchwork Empire and its position vis-à-vis Russia.

One such war for the Balkans was the taxing war with Turkey in 1877–78. Russia sprang into the conflict without assuring herself of allies or trusty well-wishers, impatiently forestalling the listless protests of the European Powers against Turkish atrocities (Disraeli played it thus, while Bismarck baited Russia onwards). The war was waged sensationally, impressing all Europe with its successes, including a winter crossing over the Balkan ridge (which brought suffering and death to numerous soldiers). Russian society, already at war with the government, uncharacteristically united with it in a patriotic uplift (both were now gripped by the fever of pan-Slavism). But the Russian advance was yet again voluntarily halted before reaching Constantinople. The Treaty of San Stefano seemingly gave the Balkans all that Russia was seeking for them: independence for Serbia, for an enlarged Montenegro, and for Romania; the expansion of Bulgaria, self-rule in Bosnia and Herzegovina, and an easing of restrictions for Christians yet remaining under Turkish rule. Triumph, then, and the realization of a century-old dream? England now directly threatened war (with her fleet at the Princes Islands), Austria—mobilisation, and all the European Powers demanded that a conference be convened to relieve Russia of her spoils. That is exactly what transpired. At the Congress of Berlin, England, having done precious little, was given Cyprus; Austria—the right to occupy Bosnia and Herzegovina; Bulgaria was once more carved up, Serbia and Montenegro carved down; while Russia herself regained only Bessarabia, which she had lost after the Crimean War. (Throughout the Congress, Gorchakov conducted himself as a weak-willed nonentity, while Disraeli was triumphantly received in England upon his return.)

Such a "victorious" war is worth no more than a lost one; cheaper yet—to not start it at all. Russian military and financial strength was undermined, the public's spirit fell; and it was then that the revolutionary era with its terrorism began to gain momentum, leading soon to the assassination of Alexander II.

In our lengthy string of emperors, **Alexander III**, unafflicted by his father's indecisiveness, was perhaps the first in a century and a half who understood the ruinous effect of both Russia's service to the interests of others and her pursuit of new conquests, understood that rule should be focused on the inner health of the nation ("the duty of Russia is first and foremost to care for herself", read the manifesto of 4 March 1881). Though Commander-in-Chief during the Turkish conflict, he did not as Emperor wage a single war (but only concluded his father's conquests in Central Asia by the peaceful acquisition of Merv, near the Afghan border; incidentally, almost bringing about a collision with England). And yet it was precisely in this war-free reign that Russia's clout abroad increased considerably. Alexander III swallowed the bitterness of Bulgarian "ingratitude": the educated Bulgarians did not appreciate in the least the enormous Russian sacrifices of the recently concluded war and hastened to free themselves from Russian influence and intervention. He likewise swallowed the bitter pill of Bismarck's betrayal, and concluded (1881) quite a balanced and wise "agreement on mutual guarantees" with Germany: had Wilhelm not abrogated it several years later, it would have precluded the possibility of a Russo–German war at the beginning of the twentieth century. After the agreement was dissolved, however, Alexander III, though carefully biding his time, had no choice but to draw closer to France.

The successful terrorism of the *narodovoltsy* in and of itself blocked for Alexander III the path to any concessions on internal policy—they would now be perceived as capitulation. Due to the implacable character of this Tsar, the murder of his father on 1 March doomed Russia to strong conservative measures during the following years, and even to the "resolution on heightened security" (1882). The composition of the soon-formed Council of Ministers hardly changed in the years of his reign, but in the interests of economy unnecessary positions at the court were abolished, as was the entire "viceregency of the Caucasus". Taxes on the peasantry were lowered, and extensions for buy-out payments were granted; Russia began exporting grain abroad and the ensuing rise in prices benefited the land-tiller. As mentioned above, Alexander III established the *zemstvo* officials (with mixed results), but weakened the peasant's role in the *zemstvo* (a significant mistake), and increased the government's control over this institution. Years passed, the situation in the country stabilised, and, it seems, the time was ripe to replace exclusively retarding measures with a multi-faceted programme of active development, for instance—the long-overdue extension of full legal rights to the peasantry. But neither the Tsar himself nor his closest advisers proposed such measures, demonstrating that they felt not the irrepressible rhythm of the age. Alexander III likewise failed to detect the worrisome deadening of the Orthodox Church, which grew ever weaker throughout the St. Petersburg period, did not provide an impetus for revivifying the Church organism or extend a helping hand to the village priests who lived in abject conditions, and abandoned the Church together with the people's faith, leaving both in the throes of a dire crisis (though one not clearly seen by all at the time). As for Muslims, in Russia they "continued to enjoy the same tolerance as before

. . . Russia had full confidence in her Muslim subjects in the Caucasus". * (And during World War I the elite regiments of Caucasian volunteers, the "indigenous division", amply substantiated this claim.)

However, the reign of Alexander III, much shorter than all the others, was tragically cut short at the height of his life and in the fullness of his spiritual strength; one cannot speculate on how he might have acted in the sharply critical period Russia was entering, or if he might have prevented it altogether. (According to Lev A. Tikhomirov, Nicholas II "from the very first day, without suspecting it in the least, began simply to dismantle everything, to break down all the foundations of his father's deeds". ¹)

By the end of the nineteenth century the Russian Empire reached its planned or, as was said at the time, "natural" (for an immense undefended plain) territorial expanse, determined on many sides by geographical boundaries. But this was a most peculiar Empire. In all the other empires then known to man, the parent state grew fat at the expense of the colonies, and nowhere existed a structure wherein the denizens of a certain colony enjoyed more rights and advantages than the inhabitants of the metropolis. But in Russia it was all backwards. Aside from Poland, who possessed a significantly more liberal constitution and order of life than Russia proper (which nonetheless did little to sweeten her subjugation), one cannot but mention the tremendous privileges enjoyed by Finland. Alexander I had granted Finns broader rights than they had enjoyed under Swedish rule; by the end of the nineteenth century, the national income had grown six- or sev-

---

* Lavisse, Rambaud, vol. 8, p. 297.
¹ *Krasny Arkhiv* journal, vol. 74, p. 175.

enfold, and Finland prospered, in large part because she was not required to pay her fair share of the Empire's expenditures. Finns were conscripted at a rate three times lower than the Russian average, so that "in a Europe armed to the teeth, Finland did less for her own defence than Switzerland" (while under Nicholas II her citizens were entirely exempt from military service and were not burdened by the First World War). In addition, "the highest echelons of Russian government were full of Finns; they held extremely important posts in the Russian army and navy, whereas Russians could hold a position or own real estate in Finland only upon becoming Finnish citizens"; "a few kilometres from their own capital, Russians were required to undergo inspection at Finnish customs . . . and speak with the officials in Finnish, for they stubbornly refused to converse in Russian."* What was the point of keeping Finland in the Empire? (Thanks to this amazing extraterritoriality and proximity to St. Petersburg, Finland became a place to regroup and an invaluable refuge for all Russian revolutionaries, including even the Socialist-Revolutionary commandos and Lenin's Bolsheviks; this served well not only the growth of terrorism and of an underground in Russia but also the unleashing of the 1905 and 1917 Revolutions.) —Although not to such a striking extent, the Asian national extremities of Russia also received enormous pecuniary transfers from the centre; and the cost of maintaining them always exceeded the income generated for the Treasury. Many of them ("Kirghizy", i.e., Kazakhs and Central Asians) were likewise exempt from conscription and were not subject to a military tax in its stead.

---

* Lavisse, Rambaud, vol. 7, pp. 417–18.

(Revolutionary propaganda joyfully celebrated the Turgai–Semirechye uprising of 1916, although it began—during World War I—in response simply to a *labour* mobilisation of the indigenous population.) The artificial transfer of resources from the centre to the periphery only exacerbated the "impoverishment of the Centre". The population which had created and maintained Russia continued to weaken. One does not find a similar phenomenon in any other European country. Dmitri I. Mendeleev (in *Towards Understanding Russia*) pointed out how much was done in Russia for the indigenous nationalities, and that it was high time attentively to take care of the Russian tribe. Yet even were this call heeded by the ruling circles, we lacked now the historical time to take action.

This picture was distinctively complemented by the extensive presence of foreign industrialists in Russia (the English on the gold fields of the Lena River; the Belgians in the ironworks of the South; Nobel in the Baku oil fields; the French in the Crimean saltworks; the Norwegians in the fishing industry of the Murmansk coastal region; the Japanese in Kamchatka and the Amur Delta; a foreign platinum syndicate; and many, many others; while in St. Petersburg itself—two-thirds of the factory owners were foreigners, and their names, the names of their factories, fill the revolutionary annals of 1917). And in Semyonov-Tian-Shansky's *Geographical Description of Our Land* the district lists of sizeable landowners are replete with foreign names.

The dense influx of foreign capitalists and industrialists can best be explained by the fact that in Russia—one cannot but be amazed!—even at the start of the twentieth century a strictly enforced income tax did not exist: a disproportionately low share (for Europe) was paid from enormous profits, an oversight exploited by rich Russians and foreigners alike, who took their scarcely depleted profits out of the country. This capital drain often caused a serious lack of funds: the incomparably wealthy Russia repeatedly solicited foreign loans (often encountering demonstrative refusals); from 1888 Russia systematically fell into arrears on her French loans, and this made her dependent on France in foreign policy, which played a role in the fateful events of summer 1914.

It was during the reign of the meek **Nicholas II**, so uncertainly feeling his way through the first years on the throne, that Russia expanded—intolerable morally and intolerable even practically!—beyond the boundless lands in her possession. Having begun from 1895 to act in concert with the European Powers in the Far East, the Russian government did not refrain (1900) from the shameful dispatch of a Russian corps to Beijing, to participate in crushing the Chinese uprising: China had grown particularly weak over the preceding decades, was almost at the point of breaking up, and all the predatory Powers eagerly took turns in exploiting her predicament. In 1898 Russia forced China to lease Port Arthur and Dalianwan, while the concession (1896) to build a railroad through Manchuria placed this region under strong Russian influence. The independence of Korea was acknowledged by the Russo–Japanese protocol of 1898, but as the Japanese penetrated Korea from the south, Nicholas II's not wholly disinterested advisers convinced him that Russia must in turn penetrate from the north. It was here that the interests of Japan collided mortally with those of Russia. Yet the path to compromise still lay open: the Japanese suggested that Russia limit herself to influence in northern Manchuria. The enemy, however, seemed so insignificant, and the experience of easy conquests had bred such arrogance. Meanwhile, Nicholas II did not sense all the vulnerable points, both domestic and external, of the not yet firm, not yet fully developed Russia (the animosity between the government on the one hand and society and the revolutionary movement on the other was far from the only weakness plaguing the State). Thus began the Japanese War, with Russia at a pernicious disadvantage from the outset: we were only just concluding the construction of the Great Siberian Railway and, because of continued competition with Austria in the Balkans, could not transfer our best troops from the Western border, sending forces of secondary quality and reserves to the Far East. In 1904, not only students, but Japanese teenagers, sought to enlist, while our students in St. Petersburg and Moscow sent telegrammes to the Mikado wishing him victory . . . Russian society, counting on sure political success (which promised even greater results than the concessions in the aftermath of the Crimean War) from Russia's humiliation, was gripped with a *craving for defeat* in this distant, unpopular, and even inexplicable war. In autumn 1905, when revolutionary flames were at their hottest, exactly one half of Nicholas II's reign was drawing to a close: in these eleven years he had nearly let all power slip from his hands, but this time Stolypin retrieved it. (At the end of the next eleven years, there was no one to repeat the feat.)

Blunders in foreign policy persisted. Wilhelm II, emphatically, almost theatrically, playing the role of intimate friend to Nicholas II (having "blessed" him to wage war in the Far East; admittedly helping by friendly neutrality), disingenuously suggested to him, at their meeting in Björkö in late 1905, that the *two* of them sign a three-way treaty of friendship with France, and the latter "would join later". Nicholas duly signed (without consulting the Council of Ministers; he later retracted his signature). Of course, quite a game was afoot to relegate France to the side; of course, Germany had in 1904 already forced an oppressive trade agreement on Russia, and it would have been difficult to count her among our friends. However, the system of a secure union with *both* Prussia *and* France—was the time-tested arrangement of Peter I; and the sharp end of the Björkö agreement was in any case pointed at England, the country which, for ninety years running, had shown persistent malevolence towards Russia, always and everywhere had sought to bring her harm, often succeeding magnificently, and only recently had allied herself with our foe in the Japanese War. Wilhelm, foreseeing a brutal war against England, was seeking to prevent conflict with Russia; and, as Continental neighbours with large armies, what a bloodbath we could have avoided in 1914 (and therefore the Revolution of 1917 as well)! It seems impossible, inexplicable that Nicholas II opted, after all, for alliance with a hater of Russia, with whom our interests had clashed so many times and in so many places. But so he did, forming the Anglo–Russian Convention of 1907, which later filled out in the Entente; the alignment of Powers in the First World War was thus fatally determined.

Soon (1909) Austria responded by annexing Bosnia and Herzegovina, while Wilhelm, in the form of an ultimatum, humiliated Russia by forcing her to *recognise* the legality of the move. True, this annexation was effectively foreordained by the Congress of Berlin (1878), but in the Russia of 1909 it was painfully received by both government and society: our fateful pan-Slavic enthusiasm cried out practically for immediate war (one impossible under Stolypin but quite promising for England).

And of course, with our pan-Slavic fervour, we could not bear the brazen Austrian ultimatum to Serbia in 1914 (precisely as Germany and Austria had calculated). And we were so readily attacked in 1914 because Russia's military might had, ever since 1904, been cast under doubt. Our troops were then thrown into Eastern Prussia in a hurried and ill-prepared sacrifice to the rescue of Paris.

Up to this point we have observed a three-hundred-year period of Russian history from the angle of missed opportunities for internal development, and the ruthless squander of national strength on the pursuit of external aims of no benefit to Russia: we troubled more about European "interests" than about our own people.

Despite all this, however, one marvels at the wealth of the people's energy, not just in Pomorye and on the Don, but, for instance, in Siberia. (The "Conquest" of Siberia, a term incorrectly used to refer to the whole of Russia's advance into this land, began with the Western Siberian episode of Yermak's clashes with the chinghisid Khan Kuchum, who had conquered the Tobolsk Tatars, and who in 1573, before Yermak's arrival on the scene, had carried out a raid on the Solikamsk region. The eighteenth century in Siberia was not marked by a large number of serious military confrontations, in contrast to the previous history of the continent—the waves of Mongolian and Turkic conquests—or when compared to the beastlike annihilation of the Maya, the North American Indians, the Patagonians, the Tasmanians. On the contrary, with the arrival of Russians, the numerous

internecine wars among the Yakuts, Buryats, Chukchi, Yukagirs and others came to an end; the Yakuts
refer to the time before the coming of Russians as the
"time of bloody battles".* Furthermore, Russians did
not impinge upon the internal structures of the ab-
original peoples, and major confrontations occurred
only with the Manchurians and the Mongols, who
impeded Russian progress in the upper Amur region.)
During the seventeenth century, a small number of
enterprising Russians opened up the enormous Siberian continent, reaching the Sea of Okhotsk, the Yana
Delta, Indigirka and the Bering (Dezhnyov) Strait,
cultivating expanses which (with the exception of some
small areas) had never before fallen under the plough;
already by the end of the seventeenth century, all
Siberia supported itself with locally grown rye. Agriculture extended as far north as Pelym, Narym, Ya-
kutsk, by the start of the eighteenth century even to
Kamchatka, and everywhere Russians and the indigenous peoples shared their hunting, agricultural and
economic experience. In 1701 we find only 25,000
Russian families inhabiting *all* of Siberia, one family
per 400 square kilometres, and in Eastern Siberia we
see villages of only one or two farmsteads. (According
to the 1719 census, 72,000 aborigines lived in Siberia,
while the Russians numbered 169,000[†], growing by
the 1780s to more than a million.) Given such a sparse
population (freemen settlers; runaway peasants allowed
to stay east of the Urals; deportees), one marvels at the
eighteenth-century Siberian example of what a people's efforts, peacefully directed at internal rather than

* *Istoriya Sibiri s drevneyshikh vremyon do nashikh dney (The History
of Siberia from Ancient Times to Our Day)*, vol. II. Leningrad: Nauka,
1968. P. 99.
† *Ibid.*, p. 55.

external tasks, can accomplish: this giant sweep of Russian labour, of unskilled trades, of an already significant industrial and metallurgical production, and of Russian commerce stretching from the Urals across all of Siberia to Kyakhta, the Chukchi Peninsula, the Aleutian Islands and Alaska (in 1787 the petty bourgeois Shelikhov founded the Russian-American Company).* In the eighteenth century, geodesic, navigational, mining and medical schools were operating in Siberia, libraries and printing houses were established, and detailed maps of the Arctic and Pacific coasts were drafted.†

Such was the wealth of the people's energy that half a century after the abolition of serfdom Russia entered a phase of torrid industrial development (ranking fifth in the world in industrial production), railroad construction, and became a major exporter of grain and (Siberian) butter. There was complete freedom for private economic activity (the same "market" which today we keep preparing to attain or adopt from abroad), as well as freedom to select both occupation and place of residence (except, of course, for the Jewish Pale of Settlement; but it too was on the wane). The large bureaucratic apparatus was closed off neither ethnically (we see representatives of many nationalities in high-level positions) nor socially (at the ministerial level we find the locomotive driver's assistant Khilkov, the peasant Rukhlov, the railway station chief Witte and the barrister's aide Krivoshein, while Generals Alexeev and Kornilov rose to military heights from the lowest social ranks.) According to Russia's last State Secretary Sergei Ye. Kryzhanovsky, Russia was an em-

* Ibid., pp. 181–282.
† Ibid., pp. 323–31, 343–53.

inently democratic country in terms of upward social mobility for separate persons: top officialdom was not composed of men of lofty birth; the Minister of Transport Krieger-Voinovsky observes that, with the exception of the peasantry's particular position, class barriers ceased to exist by the twentieth century, and "rights were determined by education, service position and type of occupation".* An independent and open court system and the strict legal basis of judicial inquest were firmly established after the 1860s, as was publication without preliminary censorship, and from 1906—a true parliament and multi-party system (for both of which we pine today as a novel achievement). Let us also note that the *zemstvo* provided free, high-quality medical care to the population. Workers' insurance was introduced. Russia had the fastest population growth and one of the best systems of women's higher education in Europe.

All this came crashing down in 1917, while the world to this day sees it in an extremely distorted light.

And yet, during this brief period (1906–13) of prosperity, perceptive minds descried the neglected illness of the state, the dangerous rift between society and government, and the decline of Russian national consciousness. Tikhomirov, at first a prominent *narodovolets* and later a theoretician of State who crossed over to the patriotic camp, wrote in his diary in 1909–10: "One can do nothing in contemporary Russia, for there *is* nothing to do. It appears we are moving towards a new revolution, and it seems inevitable . . . all, all, even singular governmental measures are as if specifically designed to bring it on"; "I am at a complete loss with Russia today. I stand atop my bastions,

* From the archives of the All-Russian Memoir Library.

do not lower my standard, fire my guns . . . but our army continues to recede and recede from me, and one cannot reasonably expect it to do anything . . ." On the youth: "Already, they are not our descendants, but rather something new"; "the Russian people! . . . it too by now has lost its former soul and feelings"* —here Tikhomirov is referring to the loss of Orthodox and national consciousness, to the "intellectual and moral decline of the nation in general".†

He correctly identified the spiritual plane of the crisis. In 1909 the question of Russian national consciousness unexpectedly became the focus of discussion among the liberal press. "When the other nationalities within the Empire set out on the path of self-determination, such a necessity arose also for the Russian individual." "In the progressive Russian press something only recently unimaginable" takes place: a "debate on the question of greater-Russian nationalism"‡, "the first sign of that consciousness which awakes as the instinct of self-preservation among peoples in times of danger". "It is no light matter that the word 'Russian' has been sullied by its transmutation into 'truly-Russian'." "Just as we ought not 'Russify' those who do not want to be 'Russified', we must not 'Rossify' ourselves, drown and lose our distinctiveness in the multinationality of Russia" (Pyotr B. Struve).§ "The attempt to greater-Russify all of Russia proved

---

* *Krasny Arkhiv*, vol. 74, pp. 165–77.

† Ibid., vol. 38.

‡ In old usage, the term "Russian" referred to all people of East Slavic stock; "greater-Russian" (*velikorusskiy*) was used as a clarification when speaking specifically of the Russian ethnicity, which lived in outer—hence "greater"—Russia. [Translator's note]

§ *Rossify* comes from the root *Rossiya* (Russia), of or pertaining to the Russian state, to the geographical entity of Russia. [Translator's note]

damaging not only to the living national traits of all the other ethnicities in the Empire but was foremost detrimental to the greater-Russian nationality itself . . . Only an intensive development directed at its own depths, a normal circulation of blood, is beneficial to the greater-Russian nationality." Society in previous years "grew ashamed not only of the false anti-national policy but also of genuine nationalism, without which national creativity cannot prosper. The people must have its own face." —"Today, as three hundred years ago, history demands from us an answer in these menacing days of trials: Do we as a distinct people have the right to an independent existence?"*

This still instructive discussion, which reads as if carried on today, did not, however, in the few remaining years before World War I, find fruitful development. The dynamic age was outpacing unhurried Russia. The rebirth of Russian national consciousness did not take place in society. In 1911, Vasily V. Rozanov put it this way: "The soul weeps: where have all the Russians gone? . . . I am terribly grieved about the Russians, for I believe that the tribe itself is dying, that everything Russian is being trampled on".†

The efforts of Orthodox society around 1905 to convene a Council and elect a Patriarch‡ were frustrated by a hampering edict of the Tsar. The Russian Orthodox Church, unfailing, was resolutely standing through to the end of her historically determined time, and Nikolai A. Berdyaev's just reproach of the intelligentsia, the democrats, and the socialists—"You

---

* The newspaper *Slovo*, 9–25 March 1909.

† *Novy Mir*, 1991, No. 3, p. 227.

‡ By decree of Peter I in 1721, the Patriarchate was abolished and replaced by a Synod of bishops, a body that would find itself subjugated by the State during its two centuries of existence. [Translator's note]

hated the Church and badgered it. You thought the people could exist without spiritual foundations, without things sacred; that material interests and education could suffice"*—falls on the heights of dozing ruling circles with its other weighty end. The Orthodox Church met the Revolution of 1917 unprepared and utterly discomposed. Only a few years later, under ferocious Bolshevik persecution, popular rebellions arose in defence of churches (1918) and, with the resolve of early Christians, tens of thousands of clergymen filed to the GULag and to death. (But the Bolshevik calculation was foolproof: these thousands were physically *subtracted* from the living opposition.)

The accumulated, unreleased national fatigue from all the previous, previous, previous Russian wars, for which the people always remained unrewarded, somehow made itself felt in World War I, and to that fatigue was added a distrust of the ruling class, amassed in generation after generation. And all of this echoed in the soldiers of a two-thousand-kilometre-long front when news of the Petrograd coup, of the sudden and complaisant abdication of the Tsar, and later of the alluring Bolshevik slogans, reached the lines.

From 1917 on, we once again began to pay, and pay in full, for all the mistakes of our history.

All the events leading up to February, the February Revolution itself, and its inexorable consequences— I have more than sufficiently expounded in *The Red Wheel*, and will omit here altogether. The Bolshevik coup was the logical and inevitable conclusion to February.

As in the preceding account we touched extensively

---

* Nikolai A. Berdyaev, *Philosophiya Neravenstva* (*The Philosophy of Inequality*). Paris: YMCA-Press, 1923. P. 20.

upon the sometimes disinterested and sometimes senseless Russian interventions into European affairs, it is appropriate here briefly to shed light on the role of the Allies in Russia's Civil War. While Germany was still resisting, the Allies naturally made efforts: first to bring the Czech corps out through Siberia, in order to use it in time against Germany, then to land in Arkhangelsk and Murmansk to prevent the Germans from doing so. But after the World War was over, the Allies lost interest in the Whites*, in the Russian generals who were their direct and personal partners in this struggle. In the North, the English were dumping ammunition and *matériel* into the sea, so as not to leave them for the Whites. White governments were not recognised (Wrangel's—only de facto, and only while he could ease the situation in Poland), but every nation splitting off from Russia was recognised immediately (and Lloyd George demanded that Kolchak follow suit). In return for military supplies, our Allies demanded Russian raw materials, grain, gold, and guarantees of debt repayment. The French (let us recall the rescue of Paris in 1914 through the sacrifice of Russian armies in Prussia) demanded that General Krasnov compensate all the losses of French enterprises in Russia, "which were incurred by the absence of order in the country", and reimburse with interest all the potential profits they had lost from 1914 onwards. In April 1920 the Allies presented Denikin and Wrangel with an ultimatum: end hostilities, "Lenin has promised an amnesty"; for assisting in the evacuation of the Crimea, the French seized Russian mil-

---

* The anti-Bolshevist coalition in the Russian Civil War (1917–22). Among the White leaders were Generals Alexeev, Denikin, Kornilov, Wrangel, and Admiral Kolchak. [Translator's note]

itary and merchant vessels, and forced Wrangel's troops being evacuated from Gallipoli to pay for their food with military property, even with stores of army underclothes. The defeat of Russia by the Bolsheviks was quite advantageous for the Allies: they would not have to share with Russia the spoils of victory. Such is the *realistic* language of international relations.

Due to the age-old underdevelopment of our concept of civil right, of our national consciousness, and owing to the fading of religious foundations over the preceding decades—our people fell into the hands of the chief Bolshevik villains as experimental sculpting material convenient for moulding into their own forms.

These lofty internationalists began headlong to palm off the lands and wealth of Russia. At the Brest negotiations they demonstrated a willingness to give away any desired tract of Russian land, so long as they themselves could hold on to power. We read in the diary of American diplomat William Bullitt of even greater concessions Lenin was offering to the American delegation in 1919: the Soviet government was prepared to give up Western Belorussia, half of the Ukraine, all of the Caucasus, the Crimea, all of the Urals, Siberia and Murmansk. "Lenin offered to limit the Communist regime to Moscow and some surrounding territory, plus the city known today as Leningrad."* (Those who today still speak rapturously of how the Bolsheviks "re-created a Great Power" would do well to recall this bellow of Lenin.) Lenin was making such a panicked offer because he feared what would have been quite a natural "Entente campaign" in defence of the Russian ally against his rebellious bunch. Soon,

* *Vremya i My*, No. 116, p. 216.

however, he grew confident that there was no such threat, and began ceding Russian lands on a smaller scale. In February 1920 he transferred to Estonia, in exchange for the first international recognition of the Soviet government, for the breach of isolation, the Russian population near Ivangorod and Narva, and "some holy places" of Pechora and Izborsk; soon thereafter he handed a sizeable Russian population over to Latvia. In pursuit of its international designs seeking the friendship of Turkey (who occupied almost all of Armenia in 1920), the Soviet government, which it would seem was still reeling from civil war in its ravaged country, began (winter 1920 to early 1921) providing extensive aid to her, sending all kind of weaponry, as well as "financial aid without indemnity" of 13 million rubles in gold (in 1922 an additional 3.5 million was provided).*

There are countless such examples. And it is doubtful if anyone has ever taken stock of the Bolshevik gang's outright theft from the vaults of the Russian state diamond fund; and of all the state, Imperial and private property it looted. Only in rare memoirs do we find descriptions of how the Kremlin storeroom treasures were, without number, literally in handfuls, pocketed away by villains and rogues for one or another Comintern† operation abroad. (The treasures of state museums were secretly sold off for similar purposes.) One could probably write an entire book on the predatory scramble for *concessions* on Russian territory: talks were held on a fifty-year (!) lease to Vanderlip of

---

* *Dokumenty vneshney politiki SSSR* (*Documents of the Foreign Policy of the USSR*), vol. III. Moscow, 1959. P. 675.

† The Communist International, a political body founded in 1919 to promote worldwide revolution. It was effectively controlled and financed by the USSR. [Translator's note]

oil fields, coal mines and fishing rights in the Primorye and Kamchatka provinces*; to the famed "anti-Soviet" Leslie Urquhart—long-term concessions on his former undertakings in the exploitation of non-ferrous metals and coal (Kyshtym, Ridder, Ekibastuz)†; to the English for twenty-five years (until 1945! . . .) the oil concessions in Baku and Grozny; to the young whippersnapper of the business world, Armand Hammer, the Alapaevsk asbestos mines (mutual heartfelt assistance and friendship with him would last until his death, already in Gorbachov's time). Not all the concessions planned at the time were realized, because the grip of Lenin's bunch on power was still regarded as rather flimsy by the West.

The history of the seventy-year-long Communist rule in the USSR, glorified by numerous bards both voluntary and bought, a rule which broke the organic flow of people's lives—is at last today bared to many in all its ugliness and abomination. As the archives are opened (if they are opened—and many have already been speedily destroyed), these seven decades will become the subject of tomes and tomes, and this essay has no room for such a survey. Let us make only the most general evaluations and observations.

All the losses suffered by our people during these examined three hundred years since the Time of Troubles pale in comparison to the losses and decline in the seventy years of Communism.

Foremost stands the physical destruction of the people. According to indirect tabulations of various statisticians, in the constant internal war waged by the

---

* *Dokumenty vneshney politiki SSSR* (*Documents of the Foreign Policy of the USSR*), vol. III. Moscow, 1959. Pp. 664–65, 676–81.

† Ibid., vol. IV, p. 774.

Soviet government against its people, the USSR lost no fewer than 45 million to 50 million people. (Professor I. A. Kurganov arrived at the figure of 66 million.) That this annihilation was not simply carried out randomly or by particular regions, but always—*selectively*, was its unmistakable stamp: it mowed down those who stood out by protest, resistance, by critical thinking, talent, or authority in their circle. Through this *counterselection* the most morally or intellectually valuable people were extirpated from the population. The average level of those who remained therefore fell irreparably; the people as a whole—declined. By the end of Stalin's epoch it had become impossible to recognise that same people which was overtaken by the Revolution: other faces, other morals, other customs, other notions.

How else but as the physical annihilation of our own people can we term the precipitate, unsparing, ruthless piling of Red Army corpses on the paths of Stalin's victories in the Soviet–German war? ("Clearing mines" with the feet of infantry thrown through the minefields is not even the most vivid example.) After Stalin's "seven million lost", after Khrushchov's "twenty million", today at last the actual figure is printed in the Russian press: 31 million. A numbing figure—one-fifth of the population! When and where had a people ever laid down so many in a war? Our "Victory" of 1945 materialised in the fortification of Stalin's dictatorship and the total depopulation of villages. The country lay as dead, and millions of lonely women could not extend the life of the nation.

But mass physical annihilation was not yet the greatest achievement of Communist rule. All those who escaped extermination were for decades bombarded by a propaganda stupefying to the mind and depraving to the soul, and all were expected to show continuously renewed signs of obedience. (The obeisant intelligentsia was further expected to weave this propaganda in detail.) From this thundering and triumphant ideological mastication, the moral and intellectual level of the population slipped further and further. (Only thus was it possible to bring up those in the elder generation today who recall as an era of happiness and prosperity the time when they gave their labour for a paltry wage, but on 7 November received half a kilo of pastries, bound with a colourful ribbon.)

However, in foreign policy—oh! here the Communists did not repeat a single blunder or flop of Tsarist diplomacy, many of which we have already noted in this essay. The Communist leaders always knew exactly what they wanted, and every action was directed exclusively towards the realization of this useful objective—never a single magnanimous or disinterested move; and every step was calculated precisely, with all possible cynicism, ruthlessness and sagacity in assessing the adversary. For the first time in the long history of Russia, its diplomacy, now Soviet, was resourceful, unyielding, tenacious, unscrupulous; it always surpassed and defeated the West. (The Communists with little effort captured those same Balkans in their entirety; took half of Europe; met no resistance in penetrating Central America, southern Africa, South Asia.) Soviet diplomacy was furnished with such ideologically attractive plumage that it won the rapturous sympathy of *progressive society* in the West, causing Western diplomats with downcast eyes to strain in their arguments to the contrary. (Let us note, however, that Soviet diplomacy likewise did not serve the interests of its own people, but pursued the alien goals of "world revolution".)

And these brilliant successes continued to stupefy and dull the weakened minds of the Soviet people with a new-baked, not national, but *Soviet patriotism*. (This is how today's aged caretakers and fervent supporters of the Great Soviet Union were raised.)

We need not repeat here the now universally known assessment of the "industrial successes" of the USSR: a lifeless economy, the deformed production of poor-quality goods not in demand, the environmental decimation of enormous expanses and the plundering exhaustion of natural resources.

Yet in all its sucking out of living juices from the population, the Soviet system did not act uniformly. According to the stringent heritage of Lenin's thought, one had to (and this was done) place the weightiest yoke on the largest and strongest republics—i.e., the Slavic ones—and especially on the "greater-Russian riff-raff" (Lenin), to subject it to the heaviest requisitions while initially relying on national minorities, Union and autonomous republics for support. It is old news today, and has been published many times, that the chief burden of the Soviet economic system was borne by the RSFSR, that disproportionately large deductions were made from its budget, that it received the smallest share of investments, while its peasants sold their produce twenty times cheaper than, say, the Georgians (potatoes versus oranges). To undermine specifically the Russian people and to exhaust precisely *its* strength was one of Lenin's undisguised objectives. Stalin continued to adhere to this policy even when he raised his acclaimed sentimental toast to the "Russian people".

In Brezhnev's era (which was sustained entirely by the parasitic pumping of crude oil abroad, to the extent that the equipment became completely worn out), new horrifying and irreversible steps were taken towards the "impoverishment of the Centre", towards the destruction of central Russia: the "closing" of thousands and thousands of "unprospective villages" (with the abandonment of many arable lands, fields and meadows), the final crushing blow to the barely breathing Russian village, disfiguring the entire face of the Russian land. And now an ominous blow to Russia herself, one which would have finished her off, was about to be leveled—the "turning back of the Russian rivers", the ultimate senile delirium of the marasmic Central Committee of the CPSU—warded off, thank God, in its last stage and at the last moment by a small courageous group of Russian writers and scientists.

The "counterselection" which the Communists conducted methodically and alertly in all social strata from their very first weeks in power, from the first days of the Cheka*, shrewdly pre-empted possible popular resistance. In the early years it would sometimes break through: the Kronstadt rebellion with the simultaneous strikes among the Petrograd proletariat, and the Tambov, Western Siberian and other peasant uprisings; all of them were providently drowned in deaths in such excess that they never rose again. And when inconvenient bumps did surface (like the 1930 weavers' strike in Ivanovo), not only did the world not hear of them, but even within the Soviet Union all news about them was reliably stifled. The people's genuine feelings towards the government could be revealed—and how visibly!—only in the years of the Soviet–German war: in the summer of 1941 alone, 3 million were easily taken prisoner; in 1943–44, entire caravans of people

---

* The first Communist secret police in Soviet Russia, a precursor of the KGB. [Translator's note]

voluntarily followed the German troops in retreat, as if they were their own . . . In the first months of the war the Soviet regime might swiftly have collapsed, freed us of itself, were it not for the racial obtuseness and arrogance of the Hitlerites, who showed our long-suffering people that they had nothing good to expect from the German invasion; only because of this did Stalin hold on. I have already written in *GULag* about the attempts to form Russian voluntary units on the German side, and of the beginnings of Vlasov's army. It is characteristic that even *in the very last months* (winter 1944–45), when it was clear to all that Hitler had lost the war, Russians who found themselves abroad sought by tens and tens of thousands to join the Russian Liberation Army!—here at last was the voice of the Russian people. And although the story of the ROA* was bespattered both by Bolshevist ideologues (with the timid Soviet *obrazovanshchina* chiming in) and by the West (where no one could imagine that Russians might have had their own aim of liberation), it will enter as a remarkable and courageous page into Russian history, in the length and future of which we believe even today. (General Vlasov is accused of not shrinking, in pursuit of Russian interests, from entering into an ostensible union with an external enemy of the state. But, as we saw, Elizabeth entered into a similar union with France and Sweden, when she moved to overthrow Biron [1740]: in both cases the enemy was too dangerous and entrenched.) In the post-Stalin era, there would blaze other brief flashes of Russian resistance—in Murom, Alexandrov, Krasnodar and especially in Novocherkassk—but they too,

---

* *Russkaya Osvoboditel'naya Armiya,* General Vlasov's Russian Liberation Army. [Translator's note]

owing to unsurpassed Bolshevist secrecy, remained unknown to the world for decades.

After all the bloody losses of the Soviet–German war, the new surge of Stalin's dictatorship, the massive swell of jail terms for all who in any way had come in contact with Europeans during the war, and after the ferocious post-war *kolkhoz** legislation (punishment for not filling the workday quota—deportation!), it seemed the end had come for the Russian people, and for those peoples with whom it shared Soviet history.

No. That was not yet the end.

We approached the end, as paradoxical as it may seem, through Gorbachov's hypocritical and irresponsible "perestroika".

There existed several reasonable paths for a gradual, careful way out from under the Bolshevik rubble. Gorbachov chose the most insincere and chaotic path. Insincere because he searched for ways to preserve both Communism, in a slightly altered form, and all the privileges of the Party *nomenklatura*. Chaotic because, with usual Bolshevik stupidity, he put forward the slogan of "acceleration", impossible and ruinous in light of the worn-out infrastructure. When "acceleration" did not yield the desired results, he dreamed up an absurd "socialist market", as a result of which industrial ties broke down and the plunder of production began. And this his "perestroika" Gorbachov coupled with "glasnost", in a short-sighted calculation of a single consequence: to win the support of the intelligentsia against the Communist die-hards who refused to recognise their own benefit from perestroika (a rearrangement of sinecures). He could not imagine in his

---

* Collective farm in the USSR. [Translator's note]

wildest dreams that by this glasnost he was flinging the doors wide open for all the fierce nationalisms. (In 1974, in the collection *From Under the Rubble,* my co-authors and I predicted that it would be very easy to set the USSR ablaze with national hatred. At the same time I warned in Stockholm: "If democracy is declared suddenly [in the USSR], we will have on our hands a multinational war of extermination, which will in an instant wash all of this democracy away". This was, however, beyond the comprehension of the CPSU leadership.) In 1990 I wrote with confidence (in *Rebuilding Russia*): "The way things are moving in our country, the 'Soviet Socialist Union' will break up *whatever* we do." (Gorbachov waxed wrathful and labeled me . . . a "monarchist". Not surprising. A leading American newspaper contributed its own comment on my phrase: "Solzhenitsyn still cannot let go of his imperial illusions"; this while they themselves feared above all the breakup of the USSR.) In the same work I warned that "we must take care not to be crushed beneath its rubble instead of gaining liberty". And this is exactly what happened: in August 1991, cement blocks rained down upon unprepared heads, while the agile fuehrers of several national republics, who for decades, until the last day, had diligently and successfully carried on in the Communist service— suddenly, in forty-eight hours, and some in twenty-four—declared themselves to be age-old ardent nationalists, patriots of their henceforth sovereign republics, and shed all their Communist birthmarks! (Their names today continue to shine upon the world's firmament, and they are respectfully welcomed in Western capitals as first-rate democrats.)

Blocks and boulders, in various areas of national life, slammed densely down in the ensuing months, pinning masses of overwhelmed people. But let us examine these sequentially.

The first consequence: the Communist Soviet Union was historically doomed, for it was founded on false ideas (most of all, it relied on an "economic basis" which proved to be its very undoing). The USSR hung on for seventy years by the fetters of an unprecedented dictatorship, but when the insides grow decrepit, all fetters fall useless.

Today not only the Party nobles, stiffened in Communist ideas, but many ordinary people, brainwashed by the thundering "Soviet patriotism", sincerely rue the breakup of the USSR: for the "USSR was the heir to the grandeur and glory of Russia", and "Soviet history was not a dead-end but a natural development" . . .

As to "grandeur and glory", we saw in our historical survey at what cost and for what alien aims we strained to the utmost in the past three hundred years. And Soviet history was precisely a d e a d - e n d . And although during those Twenties to Thirties . . . Sixties to Seventies it was *not you and I* who held power, it will be only us—who else?—who will have to answer for all the evils committed and to all the world; and let us note: o n l y   t h e   R u s s i a n s !—*here* everyone willingly yields us the exclusive and foremost position. And since the faceless and greedy pack did what it pleased, more often than not in our name, we will not be able to wash ourselves clean as quickly as the others have.

That the Soviet Empire was not only unnecessary for us, but ruinous, is a conclusion I reached in the first post-war years, in the camps. I have long believed this, for half a century. In the *Letter to the Soviet Leaders* (1973) I wrote: "The aims of a great empire and the moral health of the people are incompatible. We should not presume to invent international tasks and bear the cost of them so long as our people is in such moral disarray". In *Rebuilding Russia*: "Holding on to a great empire means to contribute to the extinction of our own people. And anyway, what need is there of this heterogeneous amalgam? Do we want Russians to lose their unique characteristics? We must strive not for the expansion of the State, but rather for the clarity of our spirit in what remains of it". We do not need to be a world arbiter, to compete for international leadership (stronger volunteers will surface); all our efforts must be directed *inwards*, towards assiduous *inner* development. The restoration of the USSR would be a sure path to crush and stifle our people for good.

We must, for once, clearly understand: Transcaucasia has its own path, separate from ours; Moldova —its own; the Baltic states—their own; not to mention Central Asia. Almost all the Central Asian leaders have already pronounced the orientation of their states towards Turkey. (Not all took note in December 1991 of the greatly promising conference held in Alma-Ata, which addressed the creation of a "Great Turan" stretching from the Anatolian peninsula to the Dzungarian Altai. In the twenty-first century, the Muslim world, growing rapidly in numbers, will doubtless undertake ambitious tasks, and—must we really meddle in that?)

The trouble is not that the USSR broke up—that was inevitable. The real trouble, and a tangle for a long time to come, is that the breakup occurred mechanically along false Leninist borders, usurping from us entire Russian provinces. In several days we lost 25 million ethnic Russians—18 percent of our entire nation—and the government could not scrape up the courage even to take note of this dreadful event, a colossal historical defeat of Russia, and to declare its political disagreement with it—at least in order to preserve the right to some kind of negotiations in the future. No . . . In the heat of the August (1991) "victory", all this was allowed to slip away. (And the national holiday of Russia became the day when the RSFSR declared its "independence", thereby severing itself from those 25 million as well . . .)

A few words on today's Ukraine. Leaving aside the swift turnabout of Ukraine's Communist chieftains, we have seen the Ukrainian nationalists, who in the past so staunchly opposed Communism, and in all, it seemed, cursed Lenin, sorely tempted from the first by his poisoned gift: eagerly accepting the false Leninist borders of Ukraine (including even the Crimean dowry of the petty tyrant Khrushchov). Ukraine (like Kazakhstan) immediately set upon a false imperial path.

I do not wish the burden of great power status upon Russia, nor upon Ukraine. I sincerely express the best wishes for the development of Ukrainian culture and distinctiveness, and genuinely love them; but why begin not with the restoration and spiritual strengthening of the national nucleus, not with cultural work within the bounds of the Ukrainian population and territory proper, but with an impulse to become a "Great Power"? I suggested (1990) solving all national, economic and cultural problems within a single Union of Eastern Slavs, and still regard this as the best solution, for I do not see any justification for splitting millions of friendship and family ties by international borders. In the same essay I stipulated that of course no one must dare forcibly to keep the Ukrainian people from secession, yet with a complete guarantee of minority rights. Do the current rulers of Ukraine and of her public opinion fully realize what a gigantic cultural task lies before them? A sizeable portion of the ethnic Ukrainian population itself does not even use or have command of the Ukrainian language. (The native language for 63 percent of the population is Russian, while ethnic Russians make up only 22 percent of the population; i.e., in Ukraine, for every Russian there are two "non-Russians" who nonetheless consider Russian to be their mother tongue!) So, the task of bringing *all* the nominal Ukrainians to use the Ukrainian language lies ahead. Next, it seems, will follow the chore of bringing Russians to speak Ukrainian (not without coercion?). The Ukrainian language has not yet grown vertically into the highest strata of science, technology and culture—this too will have to be addressed. Furthermore, Ukrainian will have to be made indispensable for international intercourse. Would not carrying out these cultural tasks require more than one century? (Meanwhile, we read accounts of discrimination against Russian schools and even kindergartens in Galicia, hooligan-like attacks on them; of the suppression in places of Russian television broadcasts; even bans on librarians to converse with readers in Russian—can this truly be the path of development for Ukrainian culture? We hear slogans like "Russians out of Ukraine!", "Ukraine for the Ukrainians!"—although numerous ethnicities populate Ukraine. Practical measures have been implemented as well: those who did not become Ukrainian citizens are experiencing constraints in employment, pensions, ownership of real estate, and are not allowed to take part in privatisation—but these people did not come to

Ukraine from abroad, they have always lived there
. . . Worse yet, anti-Russian propaganda is dissemi-
nated with a fervour difficult to understand; when taking their oath, army officers are specifically asked: "Are
you prepared to go to war with Russia?"; the army's
Socio-Psychological Agency creates the image of Russia as enemy, plays up the theme of a "military threat"
from her. And to every word uttered in Russia indi-
cating political disagreement with the cession of Russian territories to Ukraine, officials in Kiev react
hysterically: "This is war!" and "This is a shot in Sara-
jevo!"* Why does a desire for negotiations signify war?
why search out war where it does not and never will
exist?)

Nazarbaev made a faultier calculation yet in his
quest for great power status: he aimed, with the help
of the Kazakh minority, to overwhelm the *majority* of
other, entirely separate ethnicities. (And so: Russians
are removed from positions of responsibility; independent activities of Siberian and Ural Cossacks are suppressed; Orthodox churches are attacked; Russian
settlements, and now even large cities, are given Kazakh names; a period of five years is allotted for the
attainment of fluency in Kazakh—this even in areas
where 90 percent of the population is Russian. Local
television now broadcasts almost entirely in Kazakh,
although Kazakhs make up only 43 percent of the
population. What is in store for the rest was vividly
demonstrated by the perverse "elections" of 1994†. I

---

* Reference to the assassination of Austrian Archduke Franz Ferdinand,
which sparked World War I. [Translator's note]

† Reference to Kazakhstan's parliamentary elections of 7 March 1994.
An observer delegation from the Commission on Security and Cooperation
in Europe concluded on 8 March 1994 that the elections "cannot be called
free and fair". [Translator's note]

have received complaints, from local Germans*
among others, of Kazakh coercion, imperviously cov-
ered up by local authorities.) To join the concept of
the "Great Turan", while relatively easy for Central
Asia, will prove to be *quite* difficult for Kazakhstan.

As I wrote in *Rebuilding Russia*: the optimal solution is a Union of the three Slavic republics and
Kazakhstan. And judging by the press, Kravchuk
promised his colleagues at Belovezhskaya Pushcha† a
real and indissoluble union, "invisible" borders, a single army and currency. But all this soon turned out
to be a lie. Nothing of the kind was formed, and after
some time Kravchuk openly declared: "We must end
the myth of 'invisible' borders". With an important
amendment, however: asking world prices for her oil
is "blatant blackmail by Russia" (Premier Kuchma);
even "approaching world prices for oil is *economic war*"
(the Ukrainian ambassador to Moscow. Again "war".
How is it that the entire planet trades oil at world
prices and no one deems it "war"?)

Russia has truly fallen into a torn state: 25 million
have found themselves "abroad" without moving any-
where, by staying on the lands of their fathers and
grandfathers. Twenty-five million—the largest dias-
pora in the world by far; how dare we turn our back
to it??—especially since local nationalisms (which we
have grown accustomed to view as quite understandable, forgivable, and "progressive") are everywhere
suppressing and maltreating our severed compatriots.
(Those wishing to leave Central Asia, for instance, are

* Ethnic Germans have lived in the region for several centuries. [Trans-
lator's note]

† The accord forming the Commonwealth of Independent States was
signed in this town near Minsk, in December 1991. [Translator's note]

not allowed to take their personal property: such a concept does not exist, they are told.)

Rejecting, as a matter of principle, the methods of coercion and war, we can identify only the following three paths:

1) we must methodically, even if it takes quite some time, evacuate those Russians wishing to leave the Asian (Transcaucasian and Central Asian) countries, where there is likely little good in store for us—and provide quality conditions for their resettlement in Russia; for those wishing to stay behind, we must seek protection either through dual citizenship or, or . . . through the UN?—vain hope;

2) we must demand from the Baltic states unswerving and full compliance with all-European standards of national minority rights;

3) we must seek possible degrees of unification in various areas with Belarus, Ukraine and Kazakhstan, and strive, at the very least, for "invisible" borders.

And we? We have over these years hospitably found room in Russia for forty thousand Meskhetian Turks, burned out from Central Asia and rejected by Georgians from their indigenous home; for Armenians fleeing Azerbaijan; everywhere for Chechens, of course, even though they declared their independence from us; and even for Tajiks, who have a country of their own—but by no means for Russians from Tajikistan. Although they now number more than 120,000, many of them could already have been re-settled in Russia, and we would not have had to send Russian troops to defend Tajikistan from Afghanistan; it is not our business, it is not for Russians to shed blood there. (The issue of defended *borders*, of which Russia was stripped overnight, is a separate and complex matter. Yet its resolution should not be attained through Russian military presence in those republics, but rather through self-containment within the territory of Russia proper.) Was it not equally our duty to manage an evacuation of Russians from Chechnya, where they are mocked, where plunder, violence, and death threaten them at all times? And how many of our own did we take in from Tuva when Russians were being driven out?

No, in Russia we have n o r o o m for Russians, no resources—rejection.

This is both a betrayal of our own and humiliation before the entire world: who else on the planet behaves in such a manner? See how the Western countries fret and intercede for two or three of their subjects who find themselves in danger somewhere, while we—cast away 25 million and forgot about them.

We can also glean the degree of our humiliation and weakness from the implacable sentences passed on us by the West. The Helsinki Accords, which proclaimed (at the insistence of the USSR, so as to protect its European conquests) the inviolability of *international* borders, were recklessly and irresponsibly applied by Western statesmen to *internal, administrative* borders—and in their short-sighted haste, they not only ignited the protracted war of attrition in Yugoslavia (where Tito had raised up historically senseless boundaries) but helped spark many conflicts in the disintegrating Soviet Union: Sumgait, Dushanbe, Bishkek, Osh, Fergana, Mangyshlak, Nagorno-Karabakh, Ossetia, Georgia (these slaughters, let us note, did not occur inside Russia, nor were they instigated by Russians). In truth, it is not borders that should be inviolable, but the will of each nation inhabiting a particular territory. President Bush allowed himself tactlessly to interfere *before* the Ukrainian referendum, expressing sympathy for the separation of Ukraine along her Leninist borders. (Would he have said anything of the kind about Northern Ireland, for instance? . . .) The American ambassador in Kiev, Popadiuk, had the gall to declare that Sevastopol rightly belongs to Ukraine. Based on what historical erudition or relying on what legal foundations did he pronounce this learned judgement?—he failed to clarify. Why should he, when the State Department immediately supported his opinion? This—regarding Sevastopol, which even the madcap Khrushchov did not conceive of "granting" to Ukraine, for it was excluded from the Crimea as a city under Moscow's direct administrative supervision. (May one ask: what business is it of the State Department to comment on Sevastopol at all?)

The active interest of many Western politicians in the weakness of Russia and in her continued fragmentation is beyond doubt (such persistent prodding has for several years now been broadcast to our listeners by the US-sponsored Radio Free Europe). But I say with confidence that these politicians fail to see far into the twenty-first century. Circumstances will arise therein when all of Europe and the United States will be in dire need of Russia as an ally.

The second consequence of Communism's collapse in the USSR, as was hotly declared in those August days, was to be the immediate establishment of democracy. But in seventy-year-old totalitarian soil, what democracy can sprout overnight? We see too well what has sprouted in the peripheral republics. And in Russia? Only in caustic mockery can we term our system of government since 1991 as democratic; that is, as rule by the people. We do not have democracy, if only because a living, unfettered system of local self-government has not been created: it remains under the foot of those same local bosses from local Communist circles; while Moscow lies far out of earshot. Our people is by no means the master of its fate, but rather a plaything in its hands. In the provinces one hears sentiments of despair: "no one thinks of us", "no one needs us". How true. Heretofore unseen hardships have been visited upon the people, while the Communist *nomenklatura*, with Gorbachov-era experience, has skillfully and successfully adapted. Many have become "democrats", and have not suffered nearly as much as the living foundations of our country. (And the "golden children" of this *nomenklatura*, the sucklings of privileged Communist institutions, either went directly into government or, on a whim, fled to the America cursed by their fathers, even to the point of banging shoes; others yet are preparing landing pads for themselves in the West.) The executive and the so-called legislative branches fought each other for a year and a half to exhaustion, to the point of mutual debility—to the shame of an entire nation. (A paradoxical situation: the Supreme Soviet, supporters of totalitarian rule, was forced by tactical considerations to defend "democratic principles" to the utmost; while the "democrats", guided by the same tactical considerations, stood to the last for "authoritarian rule". So firmly held the convictions on each side . . .) Both parties to the struggle, irresponsibly, vying zealously with each other, flirted with the separatist tendencies of autonomous republics, thereby pushing the indignant *oblasts* and *krais* also to declare republican status; what else could they do?* And had

---

* The Federation Treaty of 1992 provided varying rights to Russia's three basic territorial units. *Autonomous republics* (thus designated due to a minority presence) were granted control over their natural resources, and

this buffoonery of dual rule continued, Russia would have fallen to pieces. (Through the "Federation Treaty", Lenin once more stings us from his Mausoleum. But Russia never was a federation, and it did not evolve as such.)

And when this crisis was settled—through blood, through the slaughter of bystanders, and again to the shame of the country—democracy flowed not from below but *from above*, from the central parliament, and along the worst channel: "party lists", with the party deciding who shall represent a particular electoral district; all this with the luxurious privileges of parliamentary deputies, and with the country still mired in destitution. Our ingrained and wretched Russian tradition: we refuse to learn how to organise *from below*, and are inclined to wait for instructions from a monarch, a leader, a spiritual or political authority—yet such are nowhere to be seen, while small-fry bustle at the heights.

The third consequence of Communism's fall was to be the return to the much-yearned-for *market*, lost since pre-revolutionary days (in our time-honoured Communist fashion, we coined a new slogan: To the shining market of the future!). Gorbachov had already dawdled for seven years, had wasted the time during which this transition could have been initiated with sensible gradualism—by the revival of the economic organism from below, from the smallest enterprises satisfying everyday necessities, allowing the people first to feed and patch themselves up; from there reform could spread higher and higher. But no, from January

given tax relief and subsidies from the central government. These privileges were not shared by the *oblasts* (provinces without minority presence) and *krais* (provinces with smaller autonomous subdivisions). [Translator's note]

1992 an armchair plan (concocted by Gaidar and the International Monetary Fund) was hastily dumped upon the country ("a hurried decision", "there was no time to select a better alternative", the President later recalled), a plan bent not on the "preservation of the people", but rather a cruel "shock" administered to it; an ignorant plan, even to the untrained eye: to "free prices" in a country lacking competition among producers; that is, giving free rein to monopolistic suppliers to raise their prices as high and for as long as they wish. (The architect of the reforms at first expressed an ill-considered hope that prices would stabilise "in . . . just two months", "in . . . just half a year"—but there was no reason for them to do so. And none found the courage to admit this short-sighted blunder.) This is when all of Communism's consequences belched back at us in full. Nothing stimulated production, it declined rapidly, prices rose sharply, the people fell into depths of indigence—and for two years now this has been the chief result of the reforms.

No, nor yet the chief. The most frightening consequence of this mindless "reform" is not even economic but psychological. The defenceless horror and confusion which have gripped our masses because of Gaidar's reform and the visible triumph of the frisky sharks of non-producing commercialism (in the folly of self-satisfaction not ashamed of flaunting their success even on television) can only be compared to Gleb Uspensky's "blow of the ruble" that proved too heavy for the post-reform peasant—from which time Russia began slowly to slip towards Catastrophe.

The most vivid reflection and assessment of our reforms can be ascertained from our demographics. Here are some statistics now known worldwide. In 1993, deaths in Russia outnumbered births by

800,000. In 1993, there were 14.6 deaths for every thousand persons, a 20 percent increase over 1992 ("reforms"!), and 9.2 births—a 15 percent decline over one year. Precisely in these last two years ("reforms"!), the suicide rate sharply increased, accounting for up to a third of all unnatural deaths. People have despaired and do not see: why live? why give birth? If in 1875 a Russian woman bore on average seven children, in pre-World War II USSR—three, as recently as five years ago—2.17; then today—she bears slightly above 1.4. We are d y i n g   o u t . Life expectancy for males has dropped to sixty, on a par with Bangladesh, Indonesia, and parts of Africa.* We read demographers: " 'I have seen the data with my own eyes . . . But even so, it is very hard to believe' "; "Russia is the first industrial country to experience such a sharp decrease in its population for reasons other than war, famine or disease"; " 'a decline in life expectancy this dramatic has never happened in the postwar world. It is truly very staggering' "; "Russia faces an [unprecedented] demographic crisis".†

The current "blow of the dollar" is yet another, yet another (and will it be the last?) retribution for our mad frenzy and crash of 1917. We are today creating a cruel, beastly, criminal society—much, much worse than the Western examples we are attempting to imitate. And anyhow, is it possible to copy a tenor of life?—it must rather blend organically with a country's traditions; Japan, for instance, did not copy, and yet entered into world civilisation without losing her distinctiveness. The national soul, to use the definition of Gustave Le Bon, consists of traditions, ideas, feel-

---

* *The New York Times*, 6 March 1994.
† Ibid.

ings and prejudices; one cannot discard all this, and there is no need to do so. For three years now, we hear of nothing save the economy. But the current crisis in our country runs much deeper than if it were only economic. It is one of consciousness and morality, and has reached such depths that we cannot surmise how many decades, even as long as a century, it will take us to stand up.

But let us focus on our theme, on the "Russian question" (I use quotes as the phrase is in such common parlance).

Russkiy or *Rossiiskiy?**

In our multinational state each term has its own intrinsic meaning, and must be adhered to. Alexander III said: "Russia must belong to the Russians." But history has matured and, a century later, it would be inaccurate to say so (or, copying the Ukrainian chauvinists—to say "Russia for the Russians"). Contrary to predictions of humanism's and internationalism's many sages, the twentieth century passed under an acute increase of national feelings throughout the planet; this process is still intensifying, and nations are resisting ubiquitous attempts to level their cultural distinctions. National consciousness must always and everywhere be respected, without exceptions. (I wrote in *Rebuilding Russia*: we must pursue "the task of consolidating a fruitful commonwealth of nations, affirming the integrity of each culture and the preservation of each language".) And *Rossiiskiy* and *Russkiy* each have particular dimensions of meaning. (Only the word

---

* Both terms mean "Russian". *Russkiy* refers to the Russian language and ethnicity; *Rossiiskiy*—to the Russian state, to geographical Russia (*Rossiya*). A citizen of Russia is a *Rossiyanin*. [Translator's note]

Rossiyanin, perhaps inevitable in official usage, somehow lacks a sonorous ring. A Mordvinian or a Chuvash
would not use it in reference to himself, but would say:
"I am a Mordvinian", "I am a Chuvash".)

We are justly reminded that on the expanses of the
Russian plain, for centuries open to all migrations, a
multitude of tribes blended with the Russian ethnicity.
But when we say "nationality", we do not mean *blood*,
but always a *spirit*, a *consciousness*, a person's orientation of preferences. Mixed blood does not determine
anything. The Russian spirit and Russian culture have
existed for centuries, and all those who feel themselves
a part of this heritage in spirit, in consciousness, in
heartfelt pain—are *Russians*.

In our time, patriotism in any peripheral former
republic is considered "progressive", and no one will
dare to term a fierce bellicose nationalism there as
"chauvinism" or, God forbid, "fascism". Russian patriotism, on the other hand, since the days of the early-
twentieth-century revolutionary democrats, has been
persistently labeled "reactionary". And any manifes-
tation of Russian national consciousness today is
sharply condemned and even hastily adjoined to "fascism" (which never existed in Russia at all, and which
in any case is not viable without a racial basis, a single-
race state).

I have had occasion to define patriotism in my essay
Repentance and Self-limitation (1973). Two decades
later I see no need to alter that definition: "Patriotism
means unqualified and unwavering love for the nation,
which implies not uncritical eagerness to serve, not
support for unjust claims, but frank assessment of its
vices and sins". Every nation has a right to *such* a
patriotism, Russia no less than any other. It is a different matter that, having survived the bloodlettings,

the losses from "counterselection", the suppression and stupefaction of consciousness, patriotism in Russia is scattered today in separate units, does not exist as a unified movement aware of itself, and many of those who call themselves "patriots" have become tarnished by leaning on Communism for support. (And some still try to raise once more, with feeble hands, the ghost of pan-Slavism, so baneful for Russia over the centuries, and entirely beyond our strength today.)

Sergei N. Bulgakov once wrote: "Those whose hearts bled with pain for their motherland were at the same time her forthright exposers. But it is only an anguished love that gives the right for this national self-castigation; yet where it does *not* exist . . . defamation of one's country, mockery of one's mother . . . elicit feelings of disgust . . ."*

I write here with this understanding and with this right.

The brief and specific survey of Russian history over the last four centuries presented above might appear as monstrously pessimistic, and the "St. Petersburg period" as unjustly discrowned, were it not for the current catatonic descent and fallen condition of the Russian people. (Charmed by the lustre of this "St. Petersburg period", understandable when seen against the backdrop of Communism, the inhabitants of the city on the Neva with great enthusiasm restored three years ago, in step neither with the twentieth century nor with our ravaged country in rags, the white starched ruff of " S a n k t -Peterburg" . . .)† H o w

---

* Sergei N. Bulgakov, "Razmyshleniya o natsional'nosti" ("Thoughts on Nationality"), in *Dva Grada*, 2nd ed. P. 289.

† *Sankt-Peterburg* (i.e., St. Petersburg) was founded by Peter I in 1703. In 1914, on account of the First World War, the Germanic-sounding "Sankt-" and "burg" were removed, and the city was known as Petrograd

d i d the once powerful Russia, overflowing with health, fall so low? T h r e e such momentous, diseased Times of Troubles—the seventeenth century, the year '17, and today—could not have just been accidents. Some fundamental flaws of State and spirit must be to blame. If for four centuries we squandered the people's strength on superfluous externalities, and in 1917 could so blindly succumb to the cheap calls to theft and desertion, must not the time to pay catch up with us? Our pitiful state today—did it not somehow amass during our history?

And thus we have come to the Great Russian Catastrophe of the 1990s. Over this century much has interlaced to precipitate it: the year 1917, seventy years of Bolshevik depravity, the millions taken onto the GULag Archipelago, and the millions unsparingly laid down at war, so that a rare Russian village welcomed back its men; and now the "blow of the Dollar", adorned by the aureole of jubilant *nouveaux riches* and thieves, roaring with laughter leveled at the people.

The Catastrophe entails above all—our dying out. These losses will only increase: how many women will risk giving birth in today's abject penury? Handicapped and sick children also will augment the Catastrophe, and their numbers are multiplying from the miserable living conditions and the boundless drunkenness of their fathers. And the utter collapse of our schools, incapable today of rearing a moral and learned generation. And a meagreness of housing conditions long forgotten by the civilised world. And the teeming grafters in government—some of whom even cheaply sell off our oil fields and rare metals in foreign concessions.

---

until 1924, when it was renamed Leningrad by the Bolsheviks. In 1991, it regained its original name. [Translator's note]

(In the end, what is there to lose, if our ancestors spilled their blood in eight exhausting wars pressing on to the Black Sea—and it all vanished overnight?) Catastrophe also in the stratification of Russians as if into two separate nations: the immense provincial-village heartland, and an entirely disparate minority in the capital, alien to it in thought and westernised in culture. Catastrophe in today's amorphous state of Russian national consciousness, in the grey indifference towards one's national affinity and an even greater apathy to compatriots in dire straits. Catastrophe also in the disfigurement of our intellect by the Soviet epoch: the deception and lie of Communism have coated our consciousness with so many layers that many cannot even discern this film over their eyes. Catastrophe in that we have too few statesmen who might simultaneously be wise, courageous, and disinterested—these three qualities, it seems, refuse to coalesce into a new Stolypin.

The character of the Russian people, so well known to our forebears, so abundantly depicted by our writers and observed by thoughtful foreigners—this character was continuously oppressed, darkened, mangled during the entire Soviet period. Openness, straightforwardness, a natural ease, a heightened simplicity, an easy disposition, a trusting resignation to fate, patience, endurance, lack of aspiration to external success, a readiness for self-reproach, for repentance, humility in heroic deeds, compassion and magnanimity—all these began to leave and seep out of our soul. The Bolsheviks harassed, exhausted and charred our character—above all, they scorched out compassion, the willingness to help others, the feeling of brotherhood; they made us more dynamic in only the bad and cruel, failing nevertheless to countervail our national flaw of life: a limited ability for independent activity and self-organisation; all this was directed by commissars in our stead.

The ruble-dollar blow of the Nineties shook our character in yet a new way: those who still preserved the kindly traits of a bygone time turned out to be the least prepared for the new way of life, helpless useless losers, unable to feed their families (a horrible feeling for parents before their own children!) and, suffocating, goggled at a new breed steamrolling over them with a new cry: "Booty! booty at any price! no matter if through fraud, rot, depravity, or the sale of Maternal wealth!" "Booty"—became the new (and how paltry) Ideology. A smashing and destructive alteration, which has as yet failed to bring any good or success to our economy and does not promise soon to do so —thickly breathed decay into the national character.

God forbid this decay become irreversible.

(All this was likewise reflected in language, the mirror of national character. Throughout the Soviet period, our compatriots unfailingly continued to lose, and now have suddenly altogether lost, the *Russian language* proper. I will not speak of stockbrokers, of hackneyed journalists, or of apartment-bound writers in the capital; but even litterateurs of peasant lineage recoil in disgust: *how* dare I draw on succulent native words, used in Russian from time immemorial? Amazingly, it is now easier for them to understand such wondrous novelties of the Russian language, rousing *no one's* censure, as "briefing," "pressing," "marketing," "rating," "holding," "voucher," "establishment," "consensus"—the list goes on. A total deafness . . .)

The "Russian question" at the end of the twentieth century stands unequivocal: Shall our people *be* or *not be*? The vulgar and insipid wave which seeks to level distinctions between cultures, traditions, nationalities and characters has engulfed the whole planet. And yet how many withstand this onslaught, unwavering and even with their head held high! Not we, however . . . If we persist in this way, who knows if in another century the time may come to cross the word "Russian" out of the dictionary?

We have a duty to escape from our current humiliating and bewildering condition, if not for ourselves, then for the memory of our forefathers and for the sake of our children and grandchildren.

Today we hear talk only of the economy, and it is true that our exhausted economy strangles us. But an economy will suffice even for a faceless ethnic material, while we must salvage also our character, our national traditions and culture, our historical path.

The Russian émigré Professor N. S. Timashev once accurately remarked: "In every condition of society there are, as a rule, several possibilities, which, becoming attainable, emerge as tendencies of societal development. Which of these tendencies are realized and which are not, cannot be forecast with absolute confidence: this depends on how they come into contact with each other. Thus, human will plays a much greater role than is afforded it by the old evolutionary"—materialistic—theory.

This—is a Christian view.

Our history appears lost to us today, but with the proper efforts of our will perhaps it only *now* begins —as sensible, directed towards its inner health, within its borders, and without veering off into the interests of others (as we have plentifully seen). Let us once again recall Uspensky's words concerning tasks before the schools: "turning an egoistic heart into an all-grieving one". We must build this kind of school: the first grade will be filled by the children of a depraved people, but the graduates will carry with them a moral spirit as they leave.

We must build a *moral* Russia, or none at all—it would not then matter anyhow. We must preserve and nourish all the good seeds which miraculously have not been trampled down in Russia. (Will the Orthodox Church help us? It was ravaged more than anything else in the Communist years. In addition, it was un- dermined internally by its three-century-long subor- dination to the State and lost the impulse for strong social actions. Now, with the active expansion into Russia of well-funded foreign confessions and sects, with the "principle of equal opportunities" for them and the impoverished Russian Church, the process of pushing Orthodoxy out of Russian life altogether has begun. Incidentally, the new explosion of materialism, this time a "capitalist" one, threatens *all* religions.)

In the numerous letters I have received from the Russian provinces, from the expanses of Russia, I have descried during these years spiritually healthy people dispersed across her breadth, often young, but dis- unified, lacking spiritual nourishment. Upon return- ing to my homeland, I hope to see many of them. Our hope is pinned precisely and exclusively on this healthy nucleus of living people. Perhaps as they grow, influence each other, and join efforts, they will grad- ually revitalise our nation.

Two and a half centuries have passed, and yet above us still looms the heritage of Shuvalov, the unfulfilled **Preservation of the People**.

There is nothing more important for us today. And in *this* lies the "Russian question" at the end of the twentieth century.

THE ROMANOV DYNASTY

Mikhail	1613–1645
Alexis	1645–1676
Fyodor II	1676–1682
Ivan V and Peter I	1682–1689
Peter I	1689–1725
Catherine I	1725–1727
Peter II	1727–1730
Anna	1730–1740
Ivan VI	1740–1741
Elizabeth	1741–1762
Peter III	1762
Catherine II	1762–1796
Paul I	1796–1801
Alexander I	1801–1825
Nicholas I	1825–1855
Alexander II	1855–1881
Alexander III	1881–1894
Nicholas II	1894–1917

ADDRESS TO THE

INTERNATIONAL ACADEMY

OF PHILOSOPHY

Leichtenstein, 14 September 1993

❧

Your Highnesses, Mr. Chairman, Ladies and Gentlemen:

Each time I arrive in the principality of Liechtenstein, I recall with emotion that outstanding lesson in courage which this tiny country and its esteemed Prince, the late Franz Joseph II, presented to the world in 1945: standing up to the relentless menace of the Soviet military machine, they did not hesitate to shelter a detachment of Russian anti-Communists seeking refuge from Stalin's tyranny.

This example is all the more instructive because in those same months the mighty democratic powers, authors of the Atlantic Charter, with its ringing promise of freedom for all the oppressed of the earth, sought to ingratiate themselves with the victorious Stalin by yielding up into slavery all of Eastern Europe, and turning over—from the West's own territory!—hundreds upon hundreds of thousands of Soviet citizens, against their expressed will, disregarding the suicides of some right there on the spot. With base force, these people were literally prodded with bayonets into

Stalin's murderous reach, towards the torments of concentration camp and death. It was appropriate that the
Soviet people lay down their lives by the millions for
the common victory with the West, but, it turned out,
they themselves did not have the right to freedom.
(And it is astonishing that the free Western press helped
to cover up this crime for twenty-five years. No one,
either at the time or later, has called those British and
American generals and administrators *war criminals*
for their deeds, much less brought them to trial.)

POLITICS AND ETHICS

This contrast between the courageous act of little
Liechtenstein and the act of betrayal in the halls of
the Great Powers naturally leads us further: what is
the role, the justifiable and necessary share of morality
in politics?

Erasmus believed politics to be an ethical category,
and called on it to manifest ethical impulses. But that,
of course, was in the sixteenth century.

And then came our Enlightenment, and by the
eighteenth century we had learned from John Locke
that it is inconceivable to apply moral terms to the
State and its actions. Politicians, who throughout history were so often free of burdensome moral constraints, had thus obtained something of an added
theoretical justification. Moral impulses among statesmen have always been weaker than political ones, but
in our time the consequences of their decisions have
grown in scale.

Moral criteria applicable to the behaviour of individuals, families and small circles certainly cannot be
transferred on a one-to-one basis to the behaviour of

states and politicians; there is no exact equivalence, as the scale, the momentum and the tasks of governmental structures introduce a certain deformation. States, however, are led by politicians, and politicians are ordinary people, whose actions have an impact on other ordinary people. Moreover, the fluctuations of political behaviour are often quite removed from the imperatives of State. Therefore, any moral demands we impose on individuals, such as understanding the difference between honesty, baseness and deception, between magnanimity, goodness, avarice and evil, must to a large degree be applied to the politics of countries, governments, parliaments and parties.

In fact, if state, party and social policy are not based on morality, then mankind has no future to speak of. The converse is true: if the politics of a state or the conduct of an individual is guided by a moral compass, this turns out to be not only the most humane but, in the long run, the most prudent behaviour for one's own future.

Among the Russian people, for one, this concept —understood as an ideal to be aimed for, and expressed by the word *truth (pravda)* and the phrase *to live by the truth (zhit' po pravde)*—has never been extinguished. And even at the murky end of the nineteenth century, the Russian philosopher Vladimir Solovyov insisted that, from a Christian point of view, moral and political activity are tightly linked, that political activity must a priori be *moral service*, whereas politics motivated by the mere pursuit of *interests* lacks any Christian content whatsoever.

Alas, in my homeland today these moral axes have fallen into even greater disuse than in the West, and I recognise the present vulnerability of my position in passing such judgements. When, in what had been the USSR, seven decades of appalling pressure were followed by the sudden and wide-open unchecked freedom to act, in circumstances of all-around poverty, the result was that many were swept down the path of shamelessness, unrestrainedly adopting the worst features of human behaviour. It must be noted here that, for seventy years, annihilation was visited upon people in our country not in a purely random fashion but was directed at those with outstanding mental and moral qualities. And so the picture in Russia today is bleaker and more savage than if it were simply the result of the general shortcomings of our human nature.

But let us not partition the misfortune between countries and nations: the misfortune is for all of us to share, as we stand at the end of Christianity's second millennium. Moreover, should we so lightly fling about this term—morality?

BENTHAM'S BEHEST

The eighteenth century left us the precept of Jeremy Bentham: morality is that which gives pleasure to the greatest number of persons; man can never desire anything except that which favours the preservation of his own existence. And the eagerness with which the civilised world took up so convenient and precious an advice was astonishing! Cold calculation holds sway in business relations, and has even become accepted as normal behaviour. To yield in some way to an opponent or competitor is considered an unforgivable blunder for the party having an advantage in position, power or wealth. The ultimate measure of every event, action or intention is a purely legalistic one. This was designed as an obstacle to immoral behaviour, and it is often successful; but sometimes, in the form of "legal realism", it facilitates precisely such behaviour.

We can only be grateful that human nature resists this legalistic hypnosis, that it does not allow itself to be lulled into spiritual lethargy and apathy towards the misfortunes of others: for many in the well-to-do West respond with spirit and warmth to far-off pain and suffering by donating goods, money, and not infrequently expending significant personal effort.

INFINITE PROGRESS

Human knowledge and human abilities continue to be perfected; they cannot, and must not, be brought to a halt. By the eighteenth century this process began to accelerate and grew more apparent. Anne-Robert-Jacques Turgot gave it the sonorous title of Progress, meaning that Progress based on economic development would inevitably and directly lead to a general mollification of the human temperament.

This resonant label was widely adopted and grew into something of a universal and proud philosophy of life: we are *progressing*! Educated mankind readily put its faith in this Progress. And yet somehow no one pressed the issue: progress yes, but *in what*? And *of what*? And might we not lose something in the course of this Progress? It was enthusiastically assumed that Progress would engulf all aspects of existence and mankind in its entirety. It was from this intense optimism of Progress that Marx, for one, concluded that history will lead us to justice without the help of God.

Time passed, and it turned out that Progress is *indeed* marching on, and is even stunningly surpassing expectations, but it is doing so only in the field of technological civilisation (with especial success in creature comforts and military innovations).

Progress has indeed proceeded magnificently, but has led to consequences which the previous generations could not have foreseen.

PROGRESS IN CRISIS

The first trifle which we overlooked and only recently discovered is that unlimited Progress cannot occur within the limited resources of our planet; that nature needs to be supported rather than conquered; that we are successfully *eating up* the environment allotted to us. (Thank heaven the alarm has been sounded, especially in developed countries, and rescue operations have begun, although on much too small a scale. And one of the most positive consequences of Communism's collapse is the disintegration of the world's most senseless, recklessly wasteful economy, a model tempting for so many nations.)

The second misjudgement turned out to be that human nature did not become gentler with Progress, as was promised. All we had forgotten was the human soul.

We have allowed our wants to grow unchecked, and are now at a loss where to direct them. And with the obliging assistance of commercial enterprises, newer and yet newer wants are concocted, some wholly artificial; and we chase after them *en masse*, but find no fulfillment. And we never shall.

The endless accumulation of possessions? That will not bring fulfillment either. (Discerning individuals have long since understood that possessions must be subordinated to other, higher principles, that they must have a spiritual justification, a mission; otherwise, as Nikolai Berdyaev put it, they bring ruin to human life, becoming the tools of avarice and oppression.)

Modern transportation has flung the world wide open to people in the West. Even without it, modern man can all but leap out beyond the confines of his being; through the eyes of television he is present throughout the whole planet all at the same time. Yet it turns out that from this spasmodic pace of techno-centric Progress, from the oceans of superficial information and cheap spectacles, the human soul does not grow, but instead grows more shallow, and spiritual life is only reduced. Our culture, accordingly, grows poorer and dimmer, no matter how it tries to drown out its decline with the din of empty novelties. As creature comforts continue to improve for the average person, so spiritual development grows stagnant. Surfeit brings with it a nagging sadness of the heart, as we sense that the whirlpool of pleasures does not bring satisfaction, and that, before long, it may suffocate us.

No, all hope cannot be pinned on science, technology, economic growth. The victory of technological civilisation has also instilled in us a spiritual insecurity. Its gifts enrich, but enslave us as well. All is *interests*, we must not neglect our *interests*, all is a struggle for material things; but an inner voice tells us that we have lost something pure, elevated and fragile. We have ceased to see *the purpose*.

Let us admit, even if in a whisper and only to ourselves: in this bustle of life at breakneck speed—*what* are we living for?

THE ETERNAL QUESTIONS REMAIN

It is up to us to stop seeing Progress (which cannot be stopped by anyone or anything) as a stream of unlimited blessings, and to view it rather as a gift from on high, sent down for an extremely intricate trial of our free will.

The gifts of the telephone and television, for instance, when used without moderation, fragment the wholeness of our time, jerking us from the natural flow of our life. The gift of lengthened life expectancy has, as one of its consequences, made the elder generation into a burden for its children, while dooming the former to a lingering loneliness, to abandonment in old age by loved ones, and to an irreparable rift from the joy of passing on their experience to the young.

Horizontal ties between people are being severed as well. With all the seeming effervescence of political and social life, alienation and apathy towards others have grown stronger in human relations. Consumed in their pursuit of material interests, people find only an overwhelming loneliness. (It is this that gave rise to the howl of existentialism.)

We must not simply lose ourselves in the mechanical flow of Progress, but strive to harness it in the interests of the human spirit; not to become the mere playthings of Progress, but rather to seek or expand ways of directing its might towards the perpetration of good.

Progress was understood to be a shining and unswerving vector, but it turned out to be a complex and twisted curve, which has once more brought us back to the very same eternal questions which loomed in earlier times, except that facing these questions then was easier for a less distracted, less disconnected man-kind.

We have lost the harmony with which we were created, the internal harmony between our spiritual and physical being. We have lost that clarity of spirit which was ours when the concepts of Good and Evil had yet to become a subject of ridicule, shoved aside by the principle of fifty-fifty.

And nothing so bespeaks the current helplessness of our spirit, our intellectual disarray, as the loss of a clear and calm attitude towards *death*. The greater his well-being, the deeper the chilling fear of death cuts into the soul of modern man. This mass fear, a fear the ancients did not know, was born of our insatiable, loud and bustling life. Man has lost the sense of him-self as a limited point in the universe, albeit one pos-sessed of free will. He began to deem himself the centre of his surroundings, adapting not himself to the world but the world to himself. And then, of course, the thought of death becomes unbearable: it is the ex-tinction of the entire universe at a stroke.

Having refused to recognise the unchanging Higher Power above us, we have filled that space with personal imperatives, and suddenly life has become a harrowing prospect indeed.

AFTER THE COLD WAR

The middle of the twentieth century passed for all of us under the cloud of the nuclear threat, a menace fierce beyond the limits of imagination. It seemed to blot out all the vices of life. Everything else seemed insignificant: we are lost for anyhow, so why not live as we please? And this great Threat also served both to halt the development of the human spirit and to postpone our reflection on the meaning of our life.

But paradoxically, this same danger temporarily gave Western society something of a unifying purpose of existence: to withstand the lethal menace of Communism. By no means did all fully understand this threat, and in no sense was this firmness equally absorbed by all in the West; there appeared not a few faint hearts thoughtlessly undermining the West's stand. But the preponderance of responsible people in government preserved the West and allowed for victory in the struggles for Berlin and Korea, for the survival of Greece and Portugal. (Yet there was a time when the Communist chieftains could have delivered a lightning blow, probably without receiving a nuclear one in return. It may be that only the hedonism of those decrepit chieftains served to postpone their scheme, until President Reagan derailed them with a new, spiraling, and ultimately unbearable arms race.)

And so, at the end of the twentieth century there burst forth a sequence of events, expected by many of my countrymen but catching many in the West by surprise: Communism collapsed due to its inherent lack of viability and from the weight of the accumulated rot within. It collapsed with incredible speed, and in a dozen countries at once. The nuclear threat suddenly was no more.

And then? A few short months of joyful relief swept over the world (while some bemoaned the death of the earthly Utopia, of the Socialist Paradise on Earth). It passed, but somehow the planet did not grow calmer; it seems instead that with a greater frequency something flares up here or explodes there; even scraping together enough UN forces for peacekeeping has become no easy task.

Besides, Communism is far from dead on the territory of the former USSR. In some republics, its institutional structures have survived in their entirety, while in all of them millions of Communist cadres remain in reserve, and its roots remain embedded in the consciousness and the daily life of the people. At the same time, under the nascent savage non-producing capitalism, ugly new ulcers have surfaced from years of torment, ushering in such repulsive forms of behaviour and such plunder of the nation's wealth as the West has not known. This, in turn, has even brought an unprepared and unprotected populace to a nostalgia for the "equality in poverty" of the past.

Although the earthly ideal of Socialism–Communism has collapsed, the problems which it purported to solve remain: the brazen use of social advantage and the inordinate power of money, which often direct the very course of events. And if the global lesson of the twentieth century does not serve as a healing inoculation, then the vast red whirlwind may repeat itself in its entirety.

The cold war is over, but the problems of modern life have been laid bare as immensely more complex than what had hitherto seemed to fit into the two dimensions of the political plane. That earlier crisis of the meaning of life and that same spiritual vacuum (which during the nuclear decades had even deepened from neglect) stand out all the more. In the era of the balance of nuclear terror this vacuum was somehow obscured by the illusion of attained stability on the planet, a stability which has proved only transitory. But now the former implacable question looms all the clearer: What is our destination?

ON THE EVE OF
THE TWENTY-FIRST CENTURY

Today we are approaching a symbolic boundary between centuries, and even millennia: less than eight
years separate us from this momentous juncture
(which, in the restless spirit of modern times, will be
proclaimed a year early, not waiting until the year
2001).

Who among us does not wish to meet this solemn
divide with exultation and in a ferment of hope? Many
thus greeted the twentieth, as a century of elevated
reason, in no way imagining the cannibalistic horrors
that it would bring. Only Dostoyevsky, it seems, fore-
saw the coming of totalitarianism.

The twentieth century did not witness a growth of
morality in mankind. Exterminations, on the other
hand, were carried out on an unprecedented scale,
culture declined sharply, the human spirit waned.
(The nineteenth century, of course, did much to pre-
pare this outcome.) So what reason have we to expect
that the twenty-first century, one bristling with first-
class weaponry on all sides, will be kinder to us?

And then there is environmental ruin. And the
global population explosion. And the colossal problem
of the Third World, still called so in quite an inade-
quate generalisation. It constitutes four-fifths of modern mankind, and soon will make up five-sixths, thus
becoming the most important component of the
twenty-first century. Drowning in poverty and misery,
it will, no doubt, soon step forward with an ever-
growing list of demands to the advanced nations. (Such
thoughts were in the air as far back as the dawn of
Soviet Communism. It is little known, for example,
that in 1921 the Tatar nationalist and Communist

Sultan Galiev called for the creation of an International of colonial and semicolonial nations, and for the establishment of its dictatorship over the advanced industrial states.) Today, looking at the growing stream of refugees bursting through all European borders, it is difficult for the West not to see itself as something of a fortress—a secure one for the time being, but clearly one besieged. And in the future, the growing ecological crisis may alter the climatic zones—leading to shortages of fresh water and arable land in places where they were once plentiful. This, in turn, may give rise to new and menacing conflicts on the planet, wars for survival.

A complex balancing act thus arises before the West. While maintaining full respect for the entire precious pluralism of world cultures and for their search for distinct social solutions, the West cannot at the same time lose sight of its own values, its historically unique stability of civic life under the rule of law—a hard-won stability which grants independence and space to every private citizen.

SELF-LIMITATION

The time is urgently upon us to limit our wants. It is difficult to bring ourselves to sacrifice and self-denial, because in political, public and private life we have long since dropped the golden key of Self-Restraint to the ocean floor. But self-limitation is the fundamental and wisest step of a man who has obtained his freedom. It is also the surest path towards its attainment. We must not wait for external events to press harshly upon us or even topple us; we must take a conciliatory stance and through prudent self-restraint learn to accept the inevitable course of events.

Only our conscience, and those close to us, know how we deviate from this rule in our personal lives. Examples of deviations from this course by larger entities—parties and governments—are in full view of all.

When a conference of the alarmed peoples of the earth convenes in the face of the unquestionable and imminent threat to the planet's environment and atmosphere, a mighty power (one consuming not much less than half of the earth's currently available resources and emitting half of its pollution) insists, because of its present-day internal interests, on lowering the demands of a sensible international agreement, as though it does not itself live on the same earth. Then other leading countries shirk from fulfilling even these reduced demands. Thus, in an economic race, we are poisoning ourselves.

Similarly, the breakup of the USSR along the fallacious Lenin-drawn borders has provided striking examples of newborn formations, which, in the pursuit of great-power imagery, rush to occupy extensive territories that are historically and ethnically alien to them—territories containing tens of thousands, or in some cases millions, of ethnically different people—giving no thought to the future, imprudently forgetting that *taking* never brings one to any good.

It goes without saying that the application of the principle of self-restraint to groups, professions, parties or entire countries, raises difficult questions which outnumber the answers already found. On this scale, all commitments to sacrifice and self-denial will have repercussions for multitudes of people who are perhaps unprepared for or opposed to them. (And even the personal self-restraint of a consumer will have an effect on producers somewhere.)

And yet, if we do not learn to limit firmly our desires and demands, to subordinate our interests to moral criteria—we, humankind, will simply be torn apart, as the worst aspects of human nature bare their teeth.

It has been pointed out by various thinkers many times (and I quote here the words of the twentieth-century Russian philosopher Nikolai Lossky): if a personality is not directed at values higher than the self, corruption and decay inevitably take hold. Or, if you will permit me to share a personal observation: we can only experience true spiritual satisfaction not in seizing, but in refusing to seize. In other words: in self-limitation.

Today it appears to us as something wholly unacceptable, constraining, even repulsive, because we have over the centuries grown unaccustomed to what for our ancestors had been a habit born of necessity. They lived with far greater external constraints, and had far fewer opportunities. The paramount importance of *self*-restraint has only in this century arisen in its pressing entirety before mankind. Yet, taking into account even the various mutual links running through contemporary life, it is nonetheless only through self-restraint that we can gradually cure both our economic and political life, albeit with much difficulty.

Today, not many will readily accept this principle for themselves. However, in the increasingly complex circumstances of our modernity, to limit ourselves is the only true path of preservation for us all.

And it helps bring back the awareness of a Whole and Higher Authority above us—and the altogether forgotten sense of humility before this Entity.

There can be only one true Progress: the sum total of the spiritual progresses of individuals; the degree of self-perfection in the course of their lives.

We were recently entertained by a naïve fable of the happy arrival at the "end of history", of the overflowing triumph of an all-democratic bliss; the ultimate global arrangement had supposedly been attained.

But we all see and sense that something very different is coming, something new, and perhaps quite stern. No, tranquillity does not promise to descend upon our planet, and will not be granted us so easily.

And yet, surely, we have not experienced the trials of the twentieth century in vain. Let us hope: we have, after all, been tempered by these trials, and our hard-won firmness will in some fashion be passed on to the following generations.

APPENDIX

This alphabetical appendix provides brief information on certain political figures, thinkers and writers who have been referred to in the text.

Berdyaev, Nikolai Aleksandrovich (1874–1948). Philosopher, religious thinker, and erstwhile Marxist.

Biron, Count **Ernst Johann von** (1690–1772). Chief adviser to and favourite of Empress Anna; a dominant figure of the 1730s and early 1740s.

Bulgakov, Sergei Nikolaevich (1871–1944). Russian theologian, ordained priest and economist.

Danilevsky, Nikolai Yakovlevich (1822–65). Philosopher and naturalist who argued that Russians and other Orthodox Slavs must pursue a path distinct from the rest of Europe.

Derzhavin, Gavriil Romanovich (1743–1816). Pre-eminent Russian poet of his era, known for a majestic, classical style; also a soldier and civil servant under Catherine II, Paul I and Alexander I.

Girai, Krym. One of the last Khans of the Crimea. A flamboyant leader, he was poisoned soon after his raids into Russia (1769).

Gorchakov, Prince **Aleksandr Mikhailovich** (1798–1883). Russian foreign minister, 1856–82. His efforts to maintain a moderate foreign policy were undone by his greatest failure, the Congress of Berlin.

Herzen, Aleksandr Ivanovich (1812–70). Writer, journalist and political thinker, famous for his memoir *My Past and Thoughts*.

Kaunitz, Count Wenzel Anton von (1711–94). Austrian statesman and diplomat; chancellor for most of Maria Theresa's reign.

Kiselyov, Pavel Dmitrievich (1788–1872). Longtime adviser to Nicholas I and member of the State Council from 1854. He is most noted for his efforts at agricultural reform.

Klyuchevsky, Vasily Osipovich (1841–1911). Perhaps Russia's most influential historian. His *History of Russia* has been noted for its attention to the social, cultural and economic aspects of history.

Kuchum. The Tatar Khan of Sibir who was defeated by Yermak.

Kurganov, Ivan Alekseevich (1895–1980). Economist who emigrated from the USSR during World War II, and later settled in America; author of books on population, the family and the state of women in the USSR.

La Harpe, Frédéric-César de (1754–1838). Swiss tutor of Alexander I.

Le Bon, Gustave (1841–1931). French psychologist who stressed the role of national character and emotions in the shaping of history.

Leskov, Nikolai Semyonovich (1831–95). Eminent Russian novelist; among his most famous works are *Cathedral Folk* and *Enchanted Wanderer*.

Levitsky, Sergei Aleksandrovich (1909–83). Emigré philosopher, essayist, and academic. Among his works is a treatise on the philosophical meaning of freedom.

Lomonosov, Mikhail Vasilyevich (1711–65). The son of a Pomorye fisherman, Lomonosov became a leading scientist and scholar. He successfully undertook a comprehensive grammatical reform of the Russian language, transformed the St. Petersburg Imperial Academy of Sciences, and founded Moscow University, which bears his name.

Lossky, Nikolai Onufrievich (1870–1965). Russian intuitionist philosopher; exiled by the Soviets in 1922. He expounded upon morality as well as psychology.

Maria Theresa (reigned 1740–80). Archduchess of Austria and Queen of Hungary and Bohemia. She ruled Austria through the War of the Austrian Succession, the Seven Years' War, the first partition of Poland, and the War of the Bavarian Succession. In her later years, she was known as an advocate for peace.

Mendeleev, Dmitri Ivanovich (1834–1907). Chemist who developed the periodic table of elements. He was also an advocate for social reform.

Moltke, Count **Helmuth von** (1800–91). A successful Prussian military leader, he also published analyses of military history.

Münnich, Count **Burkhard Christoph von** (1683–1767). Prominent political and military figure during the reign of Peter II and Anna.

Nesselrode, Count **Karl Roman Vasilyevich** (1780–1882). Russian foreign minister, 1822–56. He was relieved of his duties after Russia's defeat in the Crimean War.

Pasmanik, Daniil Samoilovich (1869–1930). Russian émigré historian.

Perovsky, Vasily Alekseevich (1794–1857). Russian general; leader of an unsuccessful campaign against Khiva and Bukhara, 1839–40.

Platonov, Sergei Fyodorovich (1860–1933). Eminent Russian historian, noted for his writings on the Time of Troubles. Convicted by the Soviets on false charges in 1930, he died in internal exile.

Poniatowski, Stanislaw II August (reigned 1764–95). King of Poland. During his reign, Poland was thrice partitioned and ceased to exist.

Rozanov, Vasily Vasilyevich (1856–1919). Philosopher, writer, literary critic.

Shamyl (1798–1871). Imam and guerrilla leader of the Chechens and other peoples of the Caucasus in their fight against the Russian forces. He was defeated in 1859.

Shuvalov, Pyotr Ivanovich (1711–62). Influential adviser to Elizabeth. Shuvalov was known as an advocate for a diminished government role in the economy.

Solovyov, Sergei Mikhailovich (1820–79). Prolific and influential Russian historian. His 29-volume *History of Russia from Ancient Times* features an unparalleled combination of meticulous detail and insightful overview.

Solovyov, Vladimir Sergeevich (1853–1900). Son of the famed historian, the younger Solovyov was a leading Russian philosopher. He tackled questions of ethics and Christianity's role in human life.

Stolypin, Pyotr Arkadievich (1862–1911). Russian prime minister, 1906–11. Noted for his efforts at land reform and crackdown on terrorism.

Struve, Pyotr Berngardovich (1870–1944). First a Marxist revolutionary, he evolved into a moderate. He fought against Bolshevik rule and emigrated to Paris.

Suvorov, Aleksandr Vasilyevich (1729–1800). Brilliant military commander under Catherine and Paul; one of a handful of generals in history never to have lost a battle. His greatest accomplishments as a strategist came in the Russo–Turkish War of 1787–90, and in the French Revolutionary Wars (1799).

Tikhomirov, Lev Aleksandrovich (1852–1923). At first a revolutionary terrorist, Tikhomirov would become a conservative journalist.

Timashev, Nikolai Sergeevich (1886–1970). Emigré professor whose works centred on sociology, law and religion.

Turgot, Anne-Robert-Jacques (1727–81). French economist of the physiocrat school of thought; civil servant under Louis XV and Louis XVI. Turgot wrote numerous economic and philosophical essays, asserting his firm belief in a perpetual progress.

Uspensky, Gleb Ivanovich (1843–1902). Writer noted for his realistic portrayal of peasant life.

Yermak Timofeevich (?–1585?). Cossack leader who invaded and established Russian control over western Siberia. He drowned in the Irtysh River.